FRENCH DISHES FOR ENGLISH TABLES

FRENCH DISHES FOR ENGLISH TABLES

BY

CLAIRE DE PRATZ

MOUNT ORLEANS
PRESS

First published 1908 by Sands & Co, London, and David McKay, Philadelphia.
Reprinted:
1925 by EP Dutton, New York, under the title *French Home Cooking*, edited by Day Monroe, reprinted December 1925 and December 1926;
1956 by EP Dutton, New York, under the title *French Home Cooking*, edited by Georgia Lingafelt;
1958 by Arco Publications Ltd, London, under the title *French Home Cooking*.

This edition published 2018 by Mount Orleans Press
23 High Street, Cricklade SN6 6AP
www.anthonyeyre.com
Volume copyright © 2018 Anthony Eyre

All rights reserved. No part of this publication may be reproduced, stored in a retrieval system, or transmitted in any form or by any means, electronic, mechanical, photocopying or otherwise, without the prior permission of the copyright holder.

CIP data for this title are available
from the British Library

Edited and produced by Anthony Eyre

ISBN 978-1-912945-00-9

Printed in Italy

CLAIRE DE PRATZ

"Swimming, walking, lying in a hammock..." – whilst Claire de Pratz's preferred recreations as listed in *Who was Who* do not really do credit to the intellectual side of her life, they are a good evocation of her elegantly hedonistic character, comfortable in her skin and secure in her independence. Well educated, both *femme de lettres* and feminist, her life reflected the Anglo-French cultural harmony of the *Entente Cordiale* and the good living of *La Belle Epoque* and the *Fin de Siècle*. Mixing easily in the artistic, literary and political salons of both Paris and London – it was to her that Oscar Wilde addressed his famous wallpaper observation, "One or the other of us has to go" – she wrote prolifically as well as pursuing a career in education and working for the French government.

Claire was born Zoé Clara Solange Cadiot in Hampstead in 1866. Her parents were French, her father, Emmanuel-Horace Cadiot, a businessman whilst her mother, Philotea Rosin de Pratz, held a professorship in French Literature at Queen's College in London. Both came from the French provinces, the father from Pillac in the Charente in the south, and the mother from Armentières in the north. They appear to have met in London, because it was in Clerkenwell that their marriage was registered in July 1865, barely six months before Claire's birth.

In an era when girls were given little education Claire was lucky to receive a good one, starting in London where she attended Queen's College, founded in 1848 and the first educational institute in the world to award academic qualifications to women. In 1881 her mother died, following which Emmanuel-Horace moved Claire and her two younger brothers, Julien and William, to Paris; it was at the Sorbonne that she continued her studies and from there that she graduated.

In her introduction to *France from Within* (1912) Claire describes her bilingual upbringing, a formal English education going hand in hand with a French domestic life; indeed, the 1871 census records the family's live-in cook Ada as being from the Seine. As Claire described, "I never remember any time of my life when I did not possess the two points of view – English and French – simultaneously, being constantly moving from one atmosphere to another". As she observed, she was both an insider and an outsider.

At around about the time of her graduation

from the Sorbonne Claire's first literary work came out, *An Iceland Fisherman* (1888), a translation of *Pêcheur d'Islande* by Pierre Loti which was published under her father's surname, Clara Cadiot. She wrote an article about Loti for *Women's World* (edited by Oscar Wilde), and at this time began a long career as a journalist, writing for the *Westminster Gazette, Daily News, Contemporary Review, Athenaeum, Petit Parisien, La Fronde* and *Revue Bleue. La Fronde* was distinguished as being the only magazine of its time entirely managed and written by women.

She also embarked on a career in teaching, starting with adult evening classes and going on to take on professorships in English at the Lycée Racine and the Lycée Lamartine in Paris. In the mid 1890s she was appointed General Inspector of Public Charities for the French Ministry of the Interior.

In the new century Claire embarked on a career as a novelist, writing *Eve Norris* (1907), *Elisabeth Davenay* (1909), *The Education of Jacqueline* (1910) and *Pomm's Daughter* (1914). With her non-fiction – *French Dishes for English Tables* (1908), *France from Within* (1912) and *A Frenchwoman's Notes on the War* (1916) – she was writing almost a book a year. The novels were well received; they are vividly written, strong on characterisation and description though the plots are rather formulaic. Their great interest lies in the fact that they draw on the events of Claire's own life, and they articulate very eloquently her beliefs and passions. Her heroines are intelligent, sensitive and independent, but are all a long way from the stereotype of the English blue-stocking of the time; as *The Oxford Companion to Edwardian Fiction* puts it, "she argues that the English are too mealy-mouthed to recognise the central importance of sex; feminists cannot be expected simply to abstain". Throughout her writing there is an attack on narrow and restrictive prejudice; in *Eve Norris* the young heroine fights against her provincial family background, "conventional, prejudiced, with no temperament at all, and weighted with the false narrow morals which are the result of generations of wrongly-applied and misunderstood puritanical principles". In *The Education of Jacqueline* the young child is brought up by her mother Francoise, who is widowed before she is thirty and finds herself "totally ignorant of life... Brought up by careful parents in view of a husband who would demand not only an innocent but also an ignorant wife...". Claire's heroines are all capable of great passion – there are passages of richly sensual purple prose, and it is interesting to see that two of the novels were published by Mills & Boon – but ultimately they are independent and confident. In *Elisabeth Davenay* the eponymous heroine is a young journalist and teacher in Paris, with many eligible admirers whom she finally rejects, wishing to avoid "spiritual bondage"; she leaves France for London where she joins the Suffragette movement. The book created a strong impression, with the *Pall Mall Gazette* commenting "*Elisabeth Davenay* is a book that every grown-up girl should read"; more thoughtfully, WT Stead wrote in "The Love Ideals of a Suffragette"

> [*Elisabeth Davenay*'s] interest, and it is a deep and absorbing interest, consists in the fact that more intrepidly than in any other English book that I have read the great question is faced and answered as to the change which the emergence of the soul and intellect of women will effect in the realm of love... The theme is handled with a boldness that never degenerates into coarseness. Although Mlle. de Pratz never flinches, she writes with delicacy that is unsullied by even a passing shadow of the impure. She is a woman handling the greatest of all woman's questions without any false shame or prudish impurity of thought...

A Frenchwoman's Notes on the War was the last book Claire wrote. *French Dishes for English Tables* was republished in New York in 1925 under the title *French Home Cooking,* with further editions coming out in New York in 1956 and in London in 1958.

Claire died on 27 March 1934.

CONTENTS.

	PAGE
Soups,	1
Sauces,	12
Fish,	20
Eggs,	48
Beef,	56
Veal,	68
Mutton,	78
Lamb,	87
Poultry,	89
Ducks,	101
Game,	107
Asparagus,	116
Artichokes,	117
Beetroots,	122
Cardoons,	124
Lettuces,	126
Onions,	127
Potatoes,	129
Peas,	133
Salsifies,	135
Sorrel,	137
Tomatoes,	138
French Beans and Scarlet-Runners,	140
Lentils,	144
Spinach,	145
Turnips,	149
Cucumbers,	151
Mushrooms,	153
Cabbages,	155
Cauliflowers,	158
Endive,	160
Carrots,	161
Celery,	163
Salads,	165
Macaroni,	168
Rice,	171
Sweet Dishes,	172

FRENCH DISHES FOR ENGLISH TABLES

POTAGES.

(SOUPS.)

There are two kinds of *potages* in French cooking —*potage gras* and *potage maigre*.

All *potages gras* are made from the *bouillon* or liquor of the *pot-au-feu*. All *potages maigres* are made with water and butter and various vegetables. The majority of English people think that soup can be good only when made with stock—which is a mistake, for all *soupes maigres* are excellent if properly cooked. A little Bovril stirred into certain *soupes maigres* just before serving is sometimes, however, a great improvement, though, of course, the soup is no longer strictly "maigre."

POTAGES GRAS.

POT-AU-FEU.

This is the national French soup—and must be made in an earthenware (*pot-au-feu*) pan with a lid, which is specially sold for the purpose.

Take three pounds of round of beef, a large marrow

bone, six carrots, some turnips, a leek or two, a bunch of parsley, a bay leaf and two or three cloves, and one lump of sugar. Put the beef into the *pot-au-feu*, and cover with as many quarts of water as there are pounds of meat; add a little salt; let it boil up, then skim very carefully, and add in a little cold water. Let it boil up again and skim once more, then add the vegetables; cover with the lid, allowing a little air in. Let it cook on a good fire constantly on boiling point for seven hours.

If the *bouillon* is required specially good, a small fowl may be cooked in the *pot-au-feu*.

When finished the meat is taken out and the liquor (*bouillon*) is poured off, skimmed, and served in a tureen with slices of bread.

The vegetables may be served in a dish and passed round with the soup.

The meat which has been cooked in the *pot-au-feu* is called *le bouilli*, and may be served with thick tomato sauce, and in many other ways. (See *Boeuf miroton, au gratin*, &c.)

POTAGE CROÛTE AU POT.
(Croûte au pot Soup.)

Fry or toast some slices of bread, pour over some good *bouillon*, and add some vegetables from the pot-au-feu.

POTAGE AU RIZ.
(Rice Soup.)

Parboil some rice, strain it off and put it into a

saucepan of boiling *bouillon*; let it simmer for twenty-five minutes, and serve.

POTAGE JULIENNE.
(Julienne Soup.)

Cut into thin strips or filaments about an inch long two carrots, two turnips, two celery heads; fry these vegetables in butter on a slow fire, stirring meanwhile, until they are very slightly browned; add two leeks likewise cut into fine strips, some chopped leaves of fresh lettuce and sorrel, a little chopped chervil, a small piece of sugar, and two tumblerfuls of stock. Let this simmer for an hour; then, if in season, add a large spoonful of green peas and asparagus tops previously boiled in water. Add the vegetables to boiling *bouillon*, and serve hot with small slices of bread.

POTAGES À LA SEMOULE ET CHIFFONADE D'OSEILLE.
(Semolina and Sorrel Soup.)

Cook some semolina in a little stock and put it into a saucepan of hot *bouillon*. Cook for ten minutes, then throw into the soup a few sorrel leaves torn from their stems and chopped up not too finely.

POTAGE AUX PÂTES D'ITALIE.
(Italian Paste Soup.)

Parboil some *pâtes d'Italie* for ten minutes in some

water. Strain off, and cook them in boiling *bouillon* for five minutes. Serve with grated parmesan.

POTAGE AU MACARONI.
(Macaroni Soup.)

This is prepared in the same manner as the *potage aux pâtes d'Italie*. (See preceding recipe.)

POTAGE AU VERMICELLE.
(Vermicelli Soup.)

This is prepared as preceding recipe.

POTAGES MAIGRES.

SOUPE-AUX-CHOUX.
(Cabbage Soup.)

Put into a large saucepan or *pot-au-feu* a cabbage cut into four, three-quarters of a pound of fat bacon, a bunch of herbs, two or three quarts of water, and pepper and salt. Let it cook for four hours. Serve the liquor in a soup tureen with some small slices of bread.

Sometimes the bacon is eaten apart, served with French mustard; the remains of the cabbage may be served around the dish. When the meat is eaten, a larger quantity may be used, a few potatoes and some haricot beans may be cooked with the dish and afterwards served with the meat.

POTAGE CRÊME D'OSEILLE.
(Cream and Sorrel Soup.)

Chop up a couple of pounds of sorrel and put it into a saucepan with three ounces of butter. Let it cook for five minutes, stirring meanwhile; dredge in a little flour, add a quart of water, and cook for half an hour. Take it off the fire, stir in a little piece of butter, bind with the yolks of three eggs and a cupful of cream. Pour it into the tureen over some slices of bread.

POTAGE SAINT-GERMAIN.
(St. Germain Soup.)

Boil a pint of split peas in a quart of water with a little salt, and let it cook for two hours. Strain the peas through a colander, put them back into their liquor and stir in a lump of butter. Add a large breakfast-cupful of plainly boiled green peas, put them into the soup; let the mixture boil up, then serve.

POTAGE-PURÉE DE HARICOTS ROUGES AU RIZ.
(Red Bean Soup.)

Put a quart of red haricots (dried beans) into a saucepan, with five quarts of water, a sprig of parsley, three onions, a little celery, two finely chopped carrots, a very little salt, two ounces of butter, and let all these ingredients cook together till the haricots are done. Strain off and pass through a colander, put back the *purée* into the liquor, and place the saucepan on a very slow fire for an hour. Then add three cupfuls of boiled rice and stir in a small lump of butter. Let it boil up, stir a little, then serve.

SOUPE-AU-LAIT.
(Milk Soup.)

Cut some small slices of bread, dredge them with a little sifted sugar, and toast them a fine brown. Put them into a soup tureen with a little salt. Take a pint and a half of boiling milk or cream, bind with the yolks of two or three eggs, and pour the mixture into the tureen over the slices of toast.

POTAGE À L'OIGNON.
(Onion Soup.)

Cut one pound of onions into thin slices and brown them in butter, add a pint and a half of water, let them cook for some time, and pass them through a colander, put the *purée* back into the liquor, stir in a lump of butter and a little Bovril or stock. Make some dice of bread sippets, and serve the soup very hot over them into the tureen.

POTAGE À LA PURÉE DE NAVETS.
(Turnip Soup.)

Peel and wash a pound of turnips. Put them into a saucepan with two quarts of water, two ounces of butter, and a little less than half a pound of rice; cook over a slow fire, stirring from time to time so that the turnips do not stick to the saucepan. When thoroughly cooked, pass them through a sieve, put back the *purée* on to the fire and add some milk, stir with a wooden spoon and let it warm up again. Just before serving, stir in another ounce of butter and a small cupful of cream. Serve with small dice sippets.

POTAGE AUX HERBES.
(Herb Soup.)

Put a large lump of butter into a saucepan; cut up a little sorrel, chervil, lettuce, and watercress. When these greens have cooked, pour over a sufficient quantity of water to make a soup, add salt and pepper and let it boil up for five minutes. Bind with the yolk of three eggs mixed with a small cupful of cream. Serve with small slices of bread.

POTAGE POMMES DE TERRE ET POIREAUX.
(Leek and Potato Soup.)

Peel and quarter six or eight large potatoes, and chop up five or six leeks, put them into a quart and a half of water with salt and pepper; boil for two hours; stir in a lump of butter, and serve with small slices of bread.

This soup may be passed through a colander before the butter is added, if desired.

POTAGE PARMENTIER.

(Potato Soup.)

Peel a dozen large potatoes, cut them into pieces, put them into a saucepan with a pint and a half of water and some pepper and salt. Let the lot cook for two or three hours; take out the potatoes and pass them through a colander; put them back into their liquor; stir in a large lump of butter; let the mixture boil up, and serve. Sprinkle a little chopped parsley or chervil over the soup before it goes to table.

POTAGE PURÉE DE TOMATE.

(Tomato Soup.)

Cut some large tomatoes, boil in water, and prepare as in preceding recipe. Add about half a pound of cold boiled rice. Let the mixture boil up and cook for another hour. Then serve.

POTAGE AU POTIRON.

(Pumpkin Soup.)

Peel, pare, and cut into dice a large slice of pumpkin, put it in a saucepan with a little water. When it is thoroughly cooked, mash it up with a fork and pass it through a colander. Mix it into a pint and a half of milk, adding a little salt and a large lump of fresh butter. Let it boil up, and pour it over small fried sippets in a tureen. A little sifted sugar may be stirred in.

POTAGE PURÉE DE CAROTTE.
(Carrot Soup.)

Slice about twelve carrots and one large potato into a quart and a half of water, add pepper and salt, and let them boil for two hours until the carrots are quite soft. Strain them out of the liquor, crush them with a fork, pass them through a colander, then put back the *purée* into the liquor, and stir in a large lump of butter and a little Bovril. Boil up and serve with fried sippets.

BOUILLABAISSE.
(Fish Soup.)

This dish is a speciality of Provence or the South of France, and is usually made with fish found only in the Mediterranean. But very good Bouillabaisse may be concocted with Northern sea fish. The following recipe is an excellent one:—

Take four and a half pounds of fish, such as gurnet, red mullet, plaice, flounder, sole, whiting, not omitting a small lobster, or even two. Cut the fish up into pieces about three or four inches square, and put them into a large saucepan or earthen pan with a pound of sliced onions, two cloves, a small bunch of parsley, two bay leaves, a sprig of thyme, two small pieces of garlic, two shallots, and two carrots, four large tablespoonfuls of olive oil, salt and peppercorns, one small chili, and two quarts of water.

Cover down the pan, and let the mixture cook for

twenty-five minutes. If whiting is used it must not be put in with the other fish and must be added ten minutes later. When the fish is cooked strain it off carefully, pass the liquor through a colander, and stir in a teaspoonful of powdered saffron.

Place some slices of slightly toasted bread in a soup tureen, pour the liquor off the Bouillabaisse over it, and serve with the fish passed round on a separate dish.

POTAGE BISQUE.

(Crayfish Soup.)

Take fifty living crayfish, or more, according to size. Wash them thoroughly, drain, then put them to cook on a good fire with some stock, without letting them float in the liquid. When sufficiently cooked, remove them from the fire and leave covered for a quarter of an hour. Then throw them into a colander and put the broth aside. When the fish are half-cold, pull off the tails; clean them well and put the pickings with the bodies into a mortar. Pound the whole to a red paste. Put the crumb of a French roll into the liquor in which the crayfish have cooked; let this mixture dry over a slow fire and then mix it in the mortar with the fish. Dilute all with a good stock; pass it through a hair sieve and place in a saucepan on the fire without letting it boil. Stir well, so that the soup is neither too clear nor too thick; salt to taste, and serve either with rice or small dice sippets.

Note.—Crayfish tails may be bought in London in tins or bottles ready prepared for cooking.

POTAGE AUX CRABES.
(Crab Soup.)

Cook twenty small crabs in salt water with some onions, fresh parsley, and some slices of carrots. Take them off the fire after twenty minutes and let them cool in their own liquor, then strain them off and pound them in a mortar with new bread crumbs and two spoonfuls of boiled rice. Moisten this paste with stock and pass it through a colander. Warm it up in the *bain-marie,* adding to it the quantity of stock necessary to make the soup.

BOUILLON DE VEAU.
(Veal Soup.)
(Broth for Invalids and Convalescents.)

Put a quarter of a pound of knuckle of veal into a small pot or saucepan; pour over it a quart of cold water; add salt, one carrot, one or two onions, a few lettuce leaves, and a little chervil. Boil slowly for an hour and a half; strain, and put aside till wanted.

SAUCES.

ROUX.
(Brown Sauce.)

Melt some butter in a saucepan and stir in some flour, so as to make a stiff paste. Place the saucepan over a quick fire and continue stirring the sauce, until it becomes a light brown. Add some stock or water, and still continue stirring until it boils. Then take it off the fire.

SAUCE BLANCHE.
(White Sauce.)

Mix an ounce of flour and half a pint of water in a saucepan. Place it on the fire and stir with a wooden spoon; add three pints of boiling water, drop by drop, and the sauce will immediately thicken. Let it cook a little; add salt and pepper and stir in a good piece of fresh butter. If the sauce were to turn, pour in a little cold water and stir very quickly. Before serving, take the saucepan off the fire and bind the sauce with the yolks of three eggs and a few drops of vinegar or lemon juice. *Sauce blanche* is better when the butter and eggs predominate over the flour. Grated nutmeg may be added.

SAUCE LIÉE À LA MAÎTRE D'HÔTEL.
(Maître d'Hôtel Sauce.)

Knead some chopped parsley into some butter and add salt, pepper, and a little vinegar. This mixture is used cold, with vegetables, fish, or cooked meat, which are hot enough to melt it.

SAUCE À LA MAÎTRE D'HÔTEL.

Make a white sauce and when boiling, add the *maître d'hôtel* in the proportion of one to five.

BEURRE FONDU.
(Melted Butter.)

Melt some butter and add salt, pepper, and a few drops of vinegar, or lemon juice.

BEURRE NOIR.

Put two ounces of butter into a frying-pan on the fire, and let it cook until it assumes a dark brown colour; take it off the fire and let it cool. Put some vinegar and pepper into another pan, let it boil down, then pour it into the cold butter. Warm up the whole together.

SAUCE HOLLANDAISE.

This is a white sauce, made without flour. Put into a bowl a quarter of a pound of fresh butter, the yolks of three eggs, some salt, and a few drops of vinegar or lemon juice. Place the bowl in a saucepan of boiling water and stir over the fire with a wooden spoon, until the sauce becomes quite thick.

SAUCE CRÊME.

This is made like the *sauce blanche*, except that *hot milk* is used instead of stock or water.

SAUCE BÉCHAMEL MAIGRE.

The same as *sauce à la crême*, to which is added two finely chopped shallots, two spring onions, and a sprig of parsley. Before serving strain through a hair sieve.

SAUCE BÉCHAMEL GRASSE.

Prepared in the same way as the *sauce blanche*, but a mixture of cream and stock is substituted for water. Two chopped shallots, spring onions, and a sprig of parsley are added with a little grated nutmeg. This sauce must be strained through a hair sieve.

SAUCE À LA DUXELLE.

Take a quarter of a pound of chopped mushrooms, some chopped parsley, two shallots, and a small piece of garlic. Add two ounces of fresh butter, an ounce of finely chopped fat bacon, two cloves and some grated nutmeg. Let this mixture cook over a slow fire, dredge with flour and add some white wine. Let it boil down to a third of its original quantity. This sauce is served with poultry or game, cooked "*en papillote*."

SAUCE PIQUANTE.

Make some brown sauce with stock or water, add a table-spoonful of chopped shallots, and three table-spoonfuls of vinegar. Season with pepper, thyme, and laurel. Let it boil up, then simmer, reduce. Add salt, if necessary.

SAUCE RAVIGOTE.

Make a brown sauce with equal quantities of white wine and stock. Let it simmer, adding one table-spoonful tarragon, spring onions, chervil, lemon juice, salt, and pepper, and serve.

SAUCE ITALIENNE.

Put a piece of butter into a saucepan, with a sprig of finely chopped parsley, one shallot, and four mushrooms. Add a little flour and some white wine. Let it boil down, then add some stock, and cook over a quick fire. Skim off the grease, and when the sauce has thickened, take it off the fire, and let it cook on the side without boiling for five minutes.

SAUCE POIVRADE.

Put a small wine-glassful of vinegar into a sauce-pan with some bay leaves, half an ounce of chopped onions, a little chopped parsley and shallots. Salt and pepper to taste. Let it boil down without burning; add a piece of butter and a spoonful of flour. Let it brown lightly and add some stock. Cook for a quarter of an hour, stirring meanwhile. Strain, then serve.

SAUCE AU BEURRE D'ANCHOIS.

Wash, scrape, and bone some anchovies; dry them, chop them up fine, and pound in a mortar; when reduced to a paste, mix with double the weight of good fresh butter. This mixture is called anchovy butter. To make it into sauce, mix it with a *roux*, made of good stock lukewarm, and mix with a wooden spoon in a saucepan before serving.

SAUCE ROBERT.

Cut up some onions into small dice, and put them into a saucepan with some butter. When half-browned, mix in some more butter; add stock and let the sauce boil for seven minutes. Skim and season. Mix in a little French mustard, and serve.

SAUCE-TOMATE.

(Tomato Sauce.)

Cut some ripe tomatoes into halves, put them into a saucepan with a few slices of lean ham, some onions cut into rings, thyme, and bay leaves. Let the mixture simmer for half an hour, and add two large table-spoonfuls of stock and a spoonful of flour. Boil until it thickens, and strain through a hair sieve. Before serving, stir in a piece of butter.

SAUCE POULETTE.

This sauce is specially used with the remains of boiled fowls. Sometimes a fowl is cooked with the *pot-au-feu*, to which it lends an excellent flavour. The fowl itself may be served with *sauce poulette*. Put in an earthen pan a large spoonful of fresh butter, into which a spoonful of flour has been mixed. The mixture must on no account be allowed to brown, and must be cooked on the edge of the fire. Stir in some colourless stock, salt to taste. Pass through a tammy and pour it over the pieces of fowl in another saucepan. Let the fowl simmer in the sauce for half an hour, adding a few mushrooms, small onions, sliced turnips, and salsifies previously parboiled in weak stock or water. Just before serving, bind with the yolks of two eggs beaten up with a large spoonful of cream and a very few drops of lemon juice or vinegar. Serve immediately.

SAUCE VERTE.

Chop up some chervil, watercress, pimpernel, tarragon, and spring onions, and pound them in a mortar. Add some olive oil, salt, pepper, and French mustard, mixing well. A few drops of vinegar may be added, if desired.

SAUCE TARTARE OU REMOULADE.

Chop up some spring onions, capers, and anchovies. Mix them with a large spoonful of French mustard seasoned with salt. Add olive oil, a few drops of vinegar, and mix thoroughly before serving. This sauce must be of the consistency of thick cream.

RÉMOULADE CHAUDE.

Chop up some parsley, spring onions, mushrooms, and a small piece of garlic; throw into a saucepan with butter. Add a little flour, and pour in two tumblerfuls of good stock and a spoonful of oil. Let it boil up, and add salt and grated nutmeg. Just before serving add a little French mustard mixed well into the sauce.

SAUCE MAYONNAISE.
(Mayonnaise Sauce.)

Mix together the yolks of two eggs, the juice of a lemon, salt, pepper, mustard, and spices; pour some oil, drop by drop, over the mixture, stirring meanwhile. If the sauce turns, add a little vinegar. The sauce must be of the consistency of thick cream. Vinegar may be added to taste. This sauce is used for fish salads, cold poultry, and vegetables. Mayonnaise sauce may also be made without the lemon, mustard, and spices.

SAUCE À L'HUILE.

Peel and pare a lemon, and remove the white skin and pips; cut it into slices, put it into a bowl with oil, vinegar, pepper, and salt, chopped parsley and tarragon. Flavour with a small chili, if desired. Mix thoroughly, and serve with a grilled fish.

SAUCE INDIENNE.

Take a piece of butter about the size of an egg, a crushed chili, and a teaspoonful of Indian saffron. Put the mixture into a saucepan and let it cook till almost fried. Make a *roux* sauce with a pint of stock, pour it into the saucepan and let the whole simmer gently. Skim the sauce. Before serving, bind it with a piece of fresh butter as large as an egg. (For recipe of *Roux* Sauce see page 12.)

SAUCE BÉARNAISE.

(Bernaise Sauce.)

Mix together a little vinegar, some chopped tarragon and chervil, the yolks of four eggs, some chopped shallots, a large piece of butter, and some pepper and salt. Simmer the mixture over the fire for ten or twelve minutes, stirring meanwhile.

FISH.

This book being specially devoted to French dishes, that is to say, *made* dishes, I refrain from giving the simpler methods of boiling, frying, grilling, &c., but may add that many of the sauces given here (see Sauces) may be used with plain, boiled, or fried fish, either cold or hot. It is perhaps necessary, however, to give here a recipe of *court-bouillon*, in which mixture French cooks boil all fresh-water fish and a great many sea-water fish, which lack distinct flavour.

COURT-BOUILLON.
(For Boiling Fish.)

Put three or four ounces of carrots, the same quantity of onions, a bunch of parsley, a sprig of thyme, and two bay leaves, twenty peppercorns, and about a spoonful of salt into a large saucepan, with two quarts of water and a tumblerful of vinegar. Let it simmer for an hour on the side of the fire, strain it off, and pour it into a deep pot, and put it aside for use.

Court-bouillon may be kept for some time if it is boiled up every four days and two tumblerfuls of water be added each time.

ANGUILLE À LA TARTARE.
(Eels à la Tartare.)

Clean and draw a large eel, then skin it. This operation is performed by soaking the eel in boiling water, the skin is then easily drawn away with a cloth. Then trim off the barbe and cut the eel into pieces about four inches long. Cook them in *court-bouillon* (see page 20) in a deep frying dish, allowing them to simmer for twenty minutes. When the eel is cooked let it cool in the liquor for twenty minutes, then strain off the pieces and wipe them in a clean cloth.

Beat two eggs in a dish with one table-spoonful of olive oil and one table-spoonful of water. Beat up as if for an omelette, dip the pieces of eel into the mixture, roll them in fine bread crumbs and fry them brown in boiling lard. Place them on a folded napkin on a dish, and garnish with fried parsley. Serve with *sauce tartare* in a sauce boat.

CARPE FRITE.
(Fried Carp.)

Cut off the gills of a carp and scrape off the scales. Divide the fish into two from the head to the tail down the back, without halving it, take out the roe, which is put on one side. Remove the liver and the bladder. Soak the fish and the roe in some milk for five minutes; salt and roll them in flour, then fry the fish in boiling fat for eight or ten minutes until quite firm and brown. Serve the fried roe in the middle of the fish with fried parsley. Garnish with lemon.

MATELOTE DE BARBILLON.
(Matelote of Barbel.)

A very good matelote may also be made of *barbel* instead of carp and eels.

MATELOTE DE CARPE ET D'ANGUILLE.
(Matelote of Carp and Eels.)

Cut a carp and an eel into pieces about two inches long. Put two ounces of butter and twenty parboiled small onions into a large saucepan. Brown the onions, then stir in a large spoonful of flour. Add one quart of red wine, a very large bunch of herbs, a large piece of garlic, salt and pepper. Cover the saucepan tightly, and let this mixture simmer for twenty minutes. Then put in the pieces of fish, laying the carp upon the eel. Add half a tumblerful of brandy, and let the fish simmer for a quarter of an hour. Then take out the garlic and the herbs and serve, pouring over the onions and the sauce.

BARBUE MARINÉE.
(Brill in Pickle.)

Draw and clean a brill, make a few gashes in its back with a sharp knife so that it may be well flavoured by the pickle. Make a pickle of vinegar, salt, peppercorns, spring onions, bay leaves, and slices of lemon. Soak the brill in the pickle for two or more hours. Strain off the fish and dip it in bread crumbs mixed with melted butter; season with a little salt and cook in the oven for fifteen minutes. Serve with a *purée* (see purée) *d'oseille*, sorrel, or of tomatoes.

BARBUE À LA PROVENÇALE.
(Brill à la Provençale.)

Serve some pieces of cold boiled brill upon a dish and garnish with thick anchovy sauce. (See sauce beurre aux anchois.)

MULET À LA MAÎTRE D'HOTEL.
(Grey Mullet à la Maître d'Hotel.)

Draw a grey mullet weighing about two pounds. Carefully scrape out the inside with a long-handled spoon and remove the scales. Then wash and dry it. Cut about a dozen gashes on each side of the fish with a long fine kitchen knife. Rub them with a little salt and pour about three spoonfuls of olive oil over them. Half an hour before serving, grill the mullets over an even moderate fire, allowing ten minutes to each side. Serve with *maître d'hotel* sauce.

MULET SAUCE HOLLANDAISE.
(Grey Mullet with Dutch Sauce.)

Mullet is also served with *sauce Hollandaise.*

The mullet must be boiled in sufficient water to cover in a small fish-kettle with a little over an ounce of salt. Cook for twenty minutes, strain off and garnish with parsley.

SOLE EN MATELOTE NORMANDE.
(Sole en Matelote Normande.)

After having emptied and prepared a fine sole, put some pieces of fresh butter into a deep fireproof china or nickel dish; add chopped parsley, some very thin slices of onions, salt and pepper. Lay in the sole and pour half a bottle of good cider or white wine over it. Garnish with a dozen oysters, a dozen trimmed mussels, and the tails of a quarter of a pint of grey shrimps. Let it cook in a slow oven, basting the fish from time to time in its own liquor. When the fish is cooked and the sauce has sufficiently simmered, serve hot.

SOLE MARGUERY.
(Marguery Soles.)

Make a *fumet de poisson* by boiling down the centre bones of some soles, with thyme, laurel, parsley, salt, and chopped mushrooms in a little water. When the whole is well cooked, pass through a very fine tammy. Line the bottom of a long oval baking dish with this *fumet* and lay in some fillets of soles; add some suet and butter and let the fish cook for ten or fifteen minutes in the oven. Then take out the fish and simmer the sauce. Stir in the beaten yolks of two eggs and a large lump of butter. Pass the sauce through a tammy, lay the fillets of sole in a *metal* baking dish, garnish with boiled mussels and shelled shrimps, pour the sauce over the whole. Let it glaze to a warm brown in the oven for a few minutes, and serve hot.

SOLES À LA PARISIENNE.
(Soles à la Parisienne.)

Draw and prepare two soles, cut off the heads and tails and put them into a deep frying-pan, sprinkle with finely chopped parsley and spring onions, salt, pepper, and grated nutmeg. Pour some warm melted butter over the whole and let the fish cook over a rather quick fire, turning them from time to time, so that they do not stick on the bottom of the pan. When cooked, serve with *Italienne* sauce. (See sauce Italienne.)

FILETS DE SOLES À L'ORLY.
(Filleted Soles à l'Orly.)

Fillet some soles and soak them in a pickle composed of lemon juice, peppercorns, and a little salt. Take them out and dip in flour; fry them in boiling fat, and serve them in a *sauce tomate*. (See sauce tomate.)

SOLES AU GRATIN.
(Soles au gratin.)

Pour some warm melted butter into a fireproof dish. Add salt and pepper, grated nutmeg, chopped mushrooms, and parsley; lay in the soles, cover them with a layer of the same ingredients, adding some pieces of butter and equal quantities of white wine and stock. Dredge with dry bread crumbs and add a little more warm melted butter. Cook till brown in a quick oven, and serve.

RAIE À LA SAINTE MÉNÉHOULD.

(Skate à la Sainte Ménéhould.)

Cut a skate into two or three pieces and soak it in the following mixture:—Work some flour into a piece of butter, put this into two pints of milk, with some parsley, a bunch of herbs, some slices of onions, and a little garlic, if desired. Flavour with sweet spices. Stir this mixture on the fire till it begins to boil, then put in the fish; when cooked strain off, scrape off the skin on both sides, and dip the pieces in some warm melted butter, dredge thickly with bread crumbs; grill over a slow fire, and serve with sauce *Robert* or a remoulade. (See Sauces.)

RAIE EN SAUCE BLANCHE.

(Skate with White Sauce.)

Wash the fish and cook it in salted water with a little vinegar and a few onions cut into slices. The liver must only cook for two or three minutes, but the rest of the fish must remain in the saucepan till it becomes soft. Then strain off the skate and skin it, and warm it up again in its own liquor passed through a tammy. Serve with caper sauce. (See sauce blanche.)

RAIE AU BEURRE NOIR.
(Skate with Black Butter.)

Cook the skate as in preceding recipe and serve with *beurre noir* sauce. (See sauce au beurre noir.) Garnish with bunches of fried parsley.

RAIE FRITE.
(Fried Skate.)

Cut the skate into fillets and soak them for four hours in a mixture composed of vinegar, sliced onions, a bunch of parsley, a bunch of sweet herbs, some chopped spring onions, a small piece of garlic, two or three cloves, peppercorns, salt, and a small piece of butter mixed with flour. Warm the mixture till the butter melts. After the fillets have soaked in the mixture, strain them off, fry over a quick fire until of a nice brown colour, and serve. Garnish with fried parsley.

COQUILLES SAINT-JACQUES.
(St. Jacques Shells.)

Cold cod or cold turbot may be boned and flaked or broken into pieces, and put into deep scallop shells. Cover with two large table-spoonfuls of béchamel or cream sauce, add salt and pepper, sprinkle with dried bread crumbs, add a small piece of butter, and brown in a quick oven.

COQUILLES MORNY.
(Morny Shells.)

These are prepared in the same manner as the *coquille St. Jacques*, by pouring the white sauce over the fish and substituting grated parmesan cheese for the bread crumbs. Brown very lightly.

THON.
(Tunny Fish.)

Tunny fish or white salmon, as it is sometimes called, abounds in the Mediterranean. It is sometimes, however, sold in London, but is generally bought in tins and preserved in oil. Here are, however, three excellent recipes.

THON FRIT.
(Fried Tunny.)

Cut the tunny into slices about two and a half inches thick, and let it soak for three hours in a mixture composed of olive oil, salt, pepper, chopped parsley, and lemon juice; then fry over a slow fire in a little oil. Brown on both sides, and serve with *remoulade* sauce. (See Sauces.)

THON GRILLÉ.
(Grilled Tunny.)

Prepare as in preceding recipe, and grill over a slow fire. Serve with *purée* of sorrel, or tomato, or *Italienne* sauce. (See Sauces.)

THON EN FRICANDEAU.

(Tunny en fricandeau.)

Lard with strips of fat bacon and cook *en fricandeau*. (See recipe, page 28.)

CABILLAUD.

(Cod Fish.)

The ordinary method of serving boiled cod fish with caper sauce or melted butter is too well known in England to give here, but there are many ways of preparing cold boiled cod. (See coquille St. Jacques and coquille morny.)

CABILLAUD À LA BÉCHAMEL.

(Cod à la Béchamel.)

Take some pieces of cold cod and warm them up in hot *béchamel* sauce. (See Sauces.) Serve with bunches of parsley.

CROQUETTES DE CABILLAUD.

(Cod Croquettes.)

Shred some cold boiled cod and mash some cold boiled potatoes with a fork. Mix in a mortar with the fish, add salt, pepper, and sweet herbs; make into balls; roll in a beaten egg and some dried bread crumbs, and fry a deep golden brown. Serve with tomato or shrimp sauce.

SALT COD FISH.

Soak the cod in fresh water for twenty-four hours, renewing the water at least three times, then thoroughly scrape the fish and put it on the fire in cold water; when cooked strain off. In a large saucepan mix a large piece of butter, pepper, grated nutmeg, chopped parsley, and spring onion, a pinch of flour, and two spoonfuls of liquor in which the fish has cooked, then put in the fish and placing the saucepan on the fire, stir unceasingly, so that the butter does not turn to oil. When the cod is quite hot, and the sauce well bound, add the juice of a lemon, and serve.

MORUE AU BEURRE NOIR.
(Cod with Black Butter.)

Cook the cod in cold water as in preceding recipe, and serve with *beurre noir*. (See Sauces.) Garnish with bunches of fried parsley.

MORUE EN BRANDADE.
(Cod en Brandade.)

Boil a fine piece of cod. Into a saucepan put a small piece of butter, a cupful of olive oil, and a little garlic if desired. Melt the mixture over a very slow fire, then shred the cod and stir it into the saucepan. From time to time add a few drops of oil, a small piece of butter and a few drops of milk. Stir all the time until the mixture becomes a thick paste. The quality of the *brandade* depends entirely upon the stirring movement, which must be gentle and continuous, and always in the same direction.

MERLANS AUX FINES-HERBES.
(Whitings and Sweet Herbs.)

Cut off the fins and tails of some fresh whiting. Cover the bottom of a deep dish with chopped parsley and spring onions, butter, salt, and grated nutmeg; lay in the whiting, cover them with melted butter, and add equal parts of white wine and stock. Cook them in a moderate oven. When the fish are half-cooked, carefully turn them over; when they are quite cooked, pour off their liquor into a small saucepan, and without removing them from the dish add some butter mixed with flour, and let them brown a little. Stir the juice of a lemon and a little pepper into the liquor in the saucepan, and serve over the fish.

MERLANS AU GRATIN.
(Whitings au gratin.)

These are prepared in exactly the same manner as *soles au gratin*. (See recipe, page 25.)

MERLANS GRILLÉS.
(Broiled Whiting.)

Prepare some whiting, season with salt and pepper, dip them in olive oil, and cook them on the grill over a slow fire, turning them several times till browned. Serve with white caper sauce or tomato sauce. (See Sauces.) Broiled whiting may also be served with slices of lemon and of gherkins.

MAQUEREAUX À LA MAÎTRE D'HÔTEL.
(Mackerel à la Maître d'Hôtel.)

Draw and clean some fine mackerel; divide them into halves lengthwise, splitting them down the back. Let them cook for half an hour in a small quantity of olive oil, salt, and a bunch of parsley, then put them on the grill, and when cooked, serve hot with a cold *maître d'hôtel* sauce (see Sauces) mixed with lemon juice.

MAQUEREAUX-ANCIENNE MODE AUX GROSEILLES VERTES.
(Mackerel with Gooseberries—old-fashioned recipe.)

Make a farce composed of half-ripe, carefully picked gooseberries, with a little cold fresh herring carefully shredded, some fresh butter, sweet herbs, salt, and cayenne pepper. Mix these ingredients well together and use the mixture to stuff two large mackerel. Cook the fish in some water with salt, butter, and a few onions; then strain them off and serve with the following sauce:—Take two handfuls of half-ripe gooseberries, split them into two and take out the pips, boil them soft in a little salted water, melt some fresh butter without letting it brown, stir in a little fresh cream and some grated nutmeg; add the boiled gooseberries and serve with the mackerel. This is an old French recipe.

VIVE OU PERCHE À LA MAÎTRE D'HÔTEL.
(Weaver or Perch à la Maître d'Hôtel.)

Prepare the fish, make a slight incision on both sides, soak them in oil with salt and parsley, and cock them on the grill. Serve with sauce *à la maître d'hôtel* or with white caper sauce. (See Sauces.)

VIVE OU PERCHE À LA NORMANDE.
(Weaver or Perch à la Normande.)

Cut off the heads and tails of the fish and lard them with filleted anchovies. Cook them in white wine, with sufficient butter, carrots, onions, parsley, cloves, thyme, and laurel to flavour. Strain the liquor through a tammy and bind with butter mixed with flour, let it simmer, then pour it over the fish with a few drops of lemon juice.

VIVE OU PERCHE À LA BORDELAISE.
(Weaver or Perch à la Bordelaise.)

This dish is prepared as *Perch à la Normande*, *Italienne* sauce being substituted for the sauce made from the liquor in which the fish have been cooked.

HARENGS FRAIS SAUCE MOUTARDE.
(Fresh Herrings à la Mustard Sauce.)

Draw and scrape some fresh herrings, let them soak

in a little oil with salt and parsley; then cook them on the grill, turning them several times till browned. Make a white sauce with butter and mix in a large spoonful of French mustard. The sauce must not boil. A simpler sauce may be made by melting a large piece of fresh butter (without allowing it to brown) into which a large spoonful of French mustard is served. In either case serve the sauce over the fish. Fresh herrings may also be served *en matelote*.

HARENGS SECS EN HORS-D'ŒUVRE.
(Dried Herrings as a *hors d'œuvre*.)

Wash some dried herrings, cut off their heads and tails, remove their skin, fins, and large centre bone. Put them to soak in equal quantities of milk and water; strain off the liquid, cut into pieces of about four inches long, and place in a deep *hors-d'œuvre* dish. Cover with a sauce *à l'huile* (see Sauces), some slices of cooked onion and of raw russet apples.

SALADE D'ANCHOIS.
(Anchovy Salad.)

Wash some anchovies in white wine, fillet them carefully and mix them in a strongly seasoned salad with lettuce or endive leaves.

ANCHOIS À LA PARISIENNE.
(Anchovies à la Parisienne.)

Soak some filleted anchovies in warm water. Meanwhile, chop up separately the whites and yolks of some hard-boiled eggs, chervil, and some pimpernel. Lay the fillets of anchovies on a hors-d'œuvre dish, arranging them in a trellis-work pattern. Fill in the spaces alternately with the whites and yolks of the eggs and green stuff. Pour a little olive oil over the whole and garnish with stoned olives, capers, and nasturtium seeds.

SARDINES FRAICHES.

Fresh sardines are not obtainable in England, as they lose all savour as soon as they leave the water, but in some parts of England pilchards may be served as sardines.

FRIED PILCHARDS.

Wipe the fish carefully, roll them in flour, and fry them in butter or good olive oil until of a nice brown colour. Serve with lemon.

CONGRE.

(Conger Eel.)

This fish must be previously boiled in good *court-bouillon* (see p. 20) before it can be cooked in other ways.

It may be prepared in the same way as cod.

HOMARD AU COURT-BOUILLON.

(Lobsters au Court-Bouillon.)

Cook a living lobster in cold salt water with a piece of fresh butter, a large bunch of parsley, a red chili,

two or three leeks, and a large tumblerful of white wine. Let it cook for twenty-five minutes and cool in the same liquor. (No *brass* saucepan must be used.) Serve the lobster with the following sauce:—
Take out the roe of the lobster and mix it with three or four spoonfuls of olive oil, a large spoonful of good French mustard, a pinch of sweet herbs, two crushed shallots, a few drops of vinegar, and the juice of a lemon.

Note.—When the lobster is bought ready cooked, it still must be prepared as directed in this recipe. (See Court-Bouillon, p. 20.)

HOMARD SAUCE-MAYONNAISE.
(Mayonnaise of Lobster.)

The lobster cooked in the above *court-bouillon* may also be served with mayonnaise sauce. (See Sauces.)

HOMARD À LA BROCHE.
(Roasted Lobster.)

Fix the lobster on to a long skewer, and put it into a Dutch oven or in the ordinary oven. Cook with a very quick fire and baste the lobster from time to time with some melted butter mixed with white wine, salt, and pepper. The lobster is cooked when the shell separates from the flesh and becomes brittle. Serve it with its own dripping mixed with the juice of a lemon, a little powdered spice and a glass of white wine.

HOMARD À L'AMERICAINE.

(Lobster à l'Americaine.)

Take the white flesh of two lobsters and cut it into pieces of half an inch thick. Cook some chopped shallots in a saucepan with some butter for two minutes, and add a glassful of white wine. Let the mixture cook, then add a little more white wine and about half a pint of thick *purée de tomate* (see recipe, p. 8) and about a quarter of a small teaspoonful of cayenne pepper. Then put in the slices of lobster and let the whole mixture reduce for ten minutes. Cut a small peeled tomato into small dice-shaped pieces, carefully removing the pips; let it simmer over a slow fire for ten minutes more, and serve in a deep dish.

HOMARD À LA PROVENÇALE.

(Lobster à la Provençale.)

Take a lobster, wrench off the pincers, and cut up the body of the fish into three or four pieces. Cook the pieces in a saucepan with some oil, salt, pepper, thyme, and bay leaf, sliced onion, and a small piece of garlic, turning the pieces from time to time. When cooked, take out the pieces of lobster and put them aside. Mix some white wine and a small glassful of brandy with the liquor that remains in the saucepan. Let the mixture simmer for ten minutes, then strain it through a sieve and warm up the pieces of lobster in the sauce before serving.

HUITRES MARINÉES.

(Pickled Oysters.)

Wash some fresh oysters and serve them in a *hors-d'œuvre* dish with the following sauce:—Mix some finely chopped shallots with vinegar, oil, pepper, sweet herbs, yolks of hard-boiled eggs, and the whites finely chopped.

MOULES À LA POULETTE.

(Mussels à la Poulette.)

Clean and wash some mussels and place them on the fire in a saucepan without adding anything to them, and as they open one by one remove one of their two shells. Then put them into another saucepan with butter, peppercorns, chopped parsley, and spring onions; stir in a little flour and add some stock and a little water. Let them boil up a few moments, and just before serving bind the sauce with yolks of eggs and the juice of one lemon.

MOULES À LA PROVENÇALE.

(Mussels à la Provençale.)

The preliminaries are the same as in preceding recipe. Put half a glassful of oil into a saucepan with chopped spring onions, parsley, and mushrooms, a small piece of chopped garlic may be added if desired. Warm up this mixture and add two large spoonfuls of stock and half the liquor first thrown off by the mussels. Let the sauce simmer for a few minutes, throw in the mussels, stir in a spoonful of good stock or gravy, and season with pepper and salt. Let it boil up again, add the juice of a lemon, and serve. The sauce must not be abundant.

MOULES À LA MARINIÈRE.
(Mussels à la Marinière.)

Put some fresh mussels into a saucepan with a piece of butter and finely chopped parsley, spring onions, garlic, and pepper, a handful of fresh bread crumbs, and boil all together for twenty minutes, and serve.

FRESH-WATER FISH.
(Sturgeon.)

The flesh of this fish is very much like veal and may be prepared in the same manner. It is rarely served whole, but, like tunny fish, is cut into thick slices.

ESTURGEON RÔTI.
(Roast Sturgeon.)

Take a large piece of sturgeon and lard it with thick strips of fat bacon. Let it soak for some time in a pickle composed of white wine, salt, peppercorns, and spices. It is then put to roast and basted with its own pickle. Serve with sauce *piquante*. (See Sauces.)

ESTURGEON BRAISÉ.
(Braised Sturgeon.)

Lard a piece of sturgeon as in preceding recipe;

put it into a saucepan with some slices of bacon and sliced onion, carrot, and parsnip, salt, pepper, spices, a bunch of herbs, and white wine. Cook over a quick fire, then let the sauce simmer for a few minutes. Serve with a sauce *piquante* (see Sauces) mixed with half the reduced sauce.

ESTURGEON AU COURT-BOUILLON.
(Sturgeon au Court-Bouillon.)

Cook the sturgeon in a *court-bouillon* (see p. 20), basting it from time to time. When cooked, strain it off, and serve with *Italienne* sauce (see Sauces) mixed with a little *court-bouillon*, a large piece of butter, and a little cayenne pepper.

ESTURGEON EN FRICANDEAU.
(Sturgeon en fricandeau.)

Lard some slices of sturgeon with thin strips of bacon, dredge with flour and brown them in boiling lard. Put the slices in a saucepan with some veal stock, mushrooms, sweet herbs, and, if in season, the hearts of some artichokes and the heads of celery. When cooked, skim the sauce, add a few drops of vinegar to it, and serve over the fish.

ESTURGEON EN MATELOTE.
(Sturgeon en Matelote.)

Cut some round slices of bread without the crust and fry them in butter; cut some thin slices of sturgeon and arrange them in a cooking dish, side by side, with salt, pepper, and butter. Let them fry for a quarter of an hour, turning, so as to cook on both sides. When done, take the slices out of the dish and stir in a little flour, some chopped parsley, spring onions, and shallots, and two glassfuls of red wine. Let the mixture boil up for a quarter of an hour, warm up the slices of fish and bread in the sauce, and serve with a sprinkling of capers.

SAUMON RÔTI.
(Roast Salmon.)

Remove the scales, lard the fish through with thin strips of bacon, and roast it in a Dutch oven. When tender, serve on a *purée d'oseille*. (See recipe, p. 137.)

SAUMON SAUTÉ.
(Fried Salmon.)

Cut and trim some salmon into thin round slices; flatten them out with the broad blade of a knife dipped into cold water. Melt some butter in a deep frying-pan, place in the slices of salmon side by side; put them on the fire and turn them from time to time. Then take out the slices of fish and keep them hot. Stir a little flour into the butter in the frying-pan, add some stock, chopped parsley, grated nutmeg, and the juice of a lemon. Pour this sauce over the slices of fish, and serve.

SAUMON FUMÉ.
(Smoked Salmon.)

Cut the smoked salmon into thin slices; place the

slices side by side in a cooking dish with some oil in the oven, turn them from time to time; when done through, strain them off, and serve with lemon juice.

ALOSE GRILLÉE À L'OSEILLE.
(Grilled Alose or Shad with Sorrel.)

Prepare in the same manner as grilled salmon.

ALOSE AU BLEU.
(Alose or Shad au bleu.)

Cook the fish in a *court-bouillon* (see p. 20). Serve on a folded napkin, with a *mayonnaise* or a sauce *à l'huile* (see Sauces) in a sauce-boat.

DORADE AU COURT-BOUILLON.
(John Dory au Court-Bouillon.)

Cook the fish in a *court-bouillon* (see p. 20) and serve with white caper sauce. (See Sauce Blanche.)

This fish may also be eaten fried or filleted, and cooked in the same manner as filleted sole.

BROCHET AU BLEU.
(Pike au bleu.)

(See Carpe au Bleu, page 43.)

FILET DE BROCHET À LA BÉCHAMEL.
(Filleted Pike à la Béchamel.)

Lay some fillets of pike in a cooking dish and cover them with reduced *béchamel* sauce (see p. 14).

Garnish with sippets of bread, pour over a little melted butter, and dredge with fine dry bread crumbs. Brown in the oven.

CARPE AU BLEU.
(Carp au bleu.)

Drain a carp, opening it as little as possible, place it in a fish-kettle with a strong boiling *court-bouillon*, made with vinegar and hardly any water. When cooked, let the fish cool in its own *court-bouillon* before serving.

TRUITE AU COURT-BOUILLON.
(Trout au Court-Bouillon.)

Tie up the head of a fine trout and cook it in a *court-bouillon*. (See recipe, p. 20.) Serve with a sauce made with some reduced *court-bouillon*, into which a large piece of butter mixed with flour is stirred.

TRUITE GRILLÉE.
(Grilled Trout.)

Prepare a trout and stuff it with seasoned butter mixed with sweet herbs. Let it soak in a pickle of white wine, lemon juice, salt and pepper, then grill it and serve with sauce *poivrade*. (See Sauces.)

BARBILLON À L'ÉTUVÉE.
(Barbel à l'étuvée.)

Draw a barbel and remove the scales. Cook it in red wine with salt, pepper, two cloves, a large bunch of herbs, and a large piece of butter. When cooked, bind the sauce with a little butter and flour, and serve.

BARBILLON AU COURT-BOUILLON.
(Barbel au Court-Bouillon.)

Draw a large barbel, but do not remove the scales until the fish is cooked. Pour some boiling vinegar over the fish and add salt and pepper. Take some wine, cloves, a bay leaf, white onions, lemon peel, a bunch of herbs, and cook the mixture in a fish-kettle. When boiling, put in the fish and allow it to boil for twenty minutes. When cooked, remove the scales off the barbel, and serve on a folded napkin. Garnish with watercress.

BARBILLON GRILLÉ.
(Grilled Barbel.)

Prepare the barbel as for *à l'etuvée*. (See recipe.) Make a few small incisions on the back of the fish, rub it over with butter and salt, and put it on the grill, turn twice, and cook for twelve minutes. When cooked, serve with sauce *aux anchois*. (See Sauces.)

When the barbel is small it may be rolled into flour and fried.

TANCHE À LA POULETTE.
(Tench à la Poulette.)

Scrape and empty some tench, cut them into pieces and brown them in butter. Stir in a spoonful of flour, add a glassful or two of white wine, salt, peppercorns, a bunch of parsley, and spring onions, thyme, bay leaf, mushrooms, and small onions. When the fish is cooked, take out the bunches of herbs, and bind the sauce with the yolk of egg. Garnish with crayfish.

TANCHE GRILLÉ.
(Grilled Tench.)

Throw the tench into boiling water and scrape with a knife from head to tail without breaking the skin. Draw them carefully, and stuff them with butter mixed with sweet herbs and a little garlic. Cook on the grill for ten minutes, and serve on a *purée de tomate,* or sauce *ravigote verte,* or sauce *Robert à la moutarde.* (See recipes.)

TANCHE AU COURT-BOUILLON.
(Tench au Court-Bouillon.)

Cook the tench in a strongly-seasoned *court-bouillon* made with wine, and serve with white caper sauce. (See Sauces.)

TANCHES FRITES.
(Fried Tench.)

Prepare as above, soaking it first for two hours in a warm pickle, composed of butter, chopped parsley and spring onions, salt, pepper, and vinegar. Wipe them, then flour, and fry them a deep brown.

ECREVISSES AU COURT-BOUILLON.
(Crayfish au Court-Bouillon.)

Before cooking crayfish, wash them in several waters and draw out the small black vein in the tail. Cook them in a *court-bouillon* composed of good white wine, or failing that, equal parts of water and vinegar, a little each of thyme, bay leaf, parsley, garlic, pepper, salt, nutmeg, onions, and sliced carrots. Let this *court-bouillon* cook for half an hour before adding the crayfish; these must cook from seven to eight minutes. Draw the saucepan off the fire and let the fish cook in the liquor. Serve in a heap on a folded napkin covered with a bed of parsley.

ECREVISSES À LA BORDELAISE.
(Crayfish à la Bordelaise.)

Cook the crayfish *au court-bouillon*. (See preceding recipe.)

Cut some carrots and onions into small dice and fry them in butter till well browned, add some white wine and a little of the *court-bouillon*. Let this sauce simmer until half its original quantity, then season strongly with chopped parsley and cayenne pepper. Warm up the crayfish in this sauce, and serve together in a vegetable-dish.

GRENOUILLES À LA POULETTE.
(Frogs à la Poulette.)

Frogs are in season in February and March. Only the back legs of the animal are eaten; these must be skinned and thrown into fresh water; then strain them off, dip in white of egg, dredge lightly with flour, and fry in butter a golden brown. Serve hot in a heap with the juice of two lemons.

EGGS.

Eggs are served on French tables at the *déjeuner*, or twelve o'clock luncheon, in a variety of forms.

Certain dishes are made in France for the cooking of eggs, which are not generally used in England.

Flat china egg-dishes, which can be used in the oven, are specially adapted for *œufs sur le plat* or *au miroir*. These are made in all sizes, capable of holding from two to six eggs. A *cocotte* egg-pan is shaped like a tiny saucepan of fireproof china. They are made in two sizes, capable of holding one or two eggs.

ŒUFS AU MIROIR OR SUR LE PLAT.
(Eggs on the Dish.)

Melt a piece of butter about the size of a walnut in a fireproof china egg-dish, break a couple of fresh eggs carefully into the butter, without breaking the yolks. Salt and pepper. Cook the dish on a quick fire or in the oven.

ŒUFS AU BEURRE-NOIR.
(Eggs with Black Butter.)

Melt two ounces of butter in a frying-pan and let

it brown, add a table-spoonful of vinegar previously warmed up. Break four eggs into an egg-dish as for *œufs au miroir*, and pour the mixture over it. Cook over a quick fire or in the oven.

ŒUFS POCHÉS AU CONSOMMÉ.
(Poached Eggs with consommé.)

Poach half a dozen eggs and slip them into a small tureen filled with strong hot *consommé*. This dish is very nourishing, and is often given to invalids.

ŒUFS SAUCE MOUTARDE.
(Eggs with Mustard Sauce.)

Make a *sauce moutarde* by melting two ounces of fresh butter; stir in gently two spoonfuls of French mustard; do not let the butter brown. Take four or six *cocotte* egg-pans and pour two teaspoonfuls of the sauce into each. Break into this a fresh egg; add salt and pepper to taste. Cook until the egg sets.

ŒUFS FRITS AUX TOMATES AND AUX OIGNONS.
(Fried Eggs with Tomatoes and Onions.)

Take two large Spanish onions; cut in thin slices and brown in two ounces of butter; add five large tomatoes cut into quarters. Let the mixture cook until the tomatoes are quite mashed. Fry some eggs on a frying-pan and lay them on this mixture. Serve hot.

ŒUFS À L'AURORE.
(Eggs à l'Aurore.)

Chop up some shallots and parsley. Mix with fine bread crumbs and season with salt and pepper.

Take some hard-boiled eggs, cut them into halves lengthwise. Take out the hard yolks, reserving the white *cups* on an egg-dish. Pound up the yolks and mix with the bread crumbs, shallots, and parsley, adding a little milk so as to form a thick paste. Refill the white *cups* with this mixture, putting what is left over around the *whites*, so as to steady them, as they must be placed cup upwards. Strew the dish with fine dry bread crumbs; put in two or three small lumps of butter, and let the eggs brown in a quick oven.

ŒUFS AUX SAUCISSES SAUCE TOMATE.
(Eggs with French Sausages and Tomato Sauce.)

Break some fresh eggs on a china egg-dish and poach. When just set, pour around the dish some good tomato sauce, and serve with a thin French sausage lightly browned, placed lengthwise over the eggs.

ŒUFS AU FROMAGE.
(Cheese Eggs.)

Break some fresh eggs into an egg-dish; pour over some thick fresh cream, season with salt and pepper, and dredge over a thick coating of grated parmesan cheese. Cook for five minutes in a hot oven. The cheese must be very hot and brown and the eggs well set.

ŒUFS À LA TRIPE.
(Eggs à la Tripe.)

Cook some slices of large onions in some butter without letting them brown. When they have become soft, stir in a little flour; add some cream, salt, and pepper, and let it simmer for five minutes. Cut some hard-boiled eggs into slices and warm them up in the mixture without letting them cook.

For four eggs use four onions and a cupful of cream.

Another method of making this dish consists in allowing the onions to brown slightly and in adding stock instead of cream.

Cucumbers may sometimes be used instead of onions; they are cut into dice, and finely chopped parsley and spring onions are added, cream and stock are stirred in in equal quantities.

ŒUFS BROUILLÉS.
(Scrambled Eggs.)

Butter an egg-dish, add salt and pepper and a little milk; break in some eggs; put the egg-dish on the fire, beat up the eggs quickly, and when they begin to cook draw the dish on to the side of the fire, stirring them meanwhile. Serve with finely chopped parsley. *Œufs brouillés* may be made with asparagus tops, slices of truffles, or mushrooms, or grated parmesan cheese. The ingredients are put into the dish just before the eggs, and are stirred into the eggs during the process of cooking.

ŒUFS À LA BÉCHAMEL.
(Eggs à la Béchamel.)

Take some hard-boiled eggs, cut them into halves lengthwise, put them into a deep egg-dish and pour over them some hot sauce *à la crême*, and serve. A little grated parmesan cheese may be sprinkled over the top and browned in the oven. This is a great improvement.

ŒUFS DURS A L'OSEILLE.
(Hard boiled Eggs and Sorrel.)

Take a pound and a half of sorrel, as fresh and as green as possible, tear the leaves off the stalks and throw them into a pan of cold water; wash thoroughly, then strain off. Put the leaves into a large saucepan with a little salt and a quart of water. Cook this for a quarter of an hour, stirring meanwhile with a wooden spoon; then strain off the sorrel and chop it up fine. Put it into a smaller saucepan with two ounces of butter and two large spoonfuls of flour. Stir it thoroughly, adding a tumblerful of stock, and let it cook for half an hour, stirring from time to time. Serve on a hot dish; on the bed of sorrel lay some hard-boiled eggs cut lengthwise, placing the yolk upward.

OMELETTES.

Omelettes are essentially a French dish, and though very simple are not easy to make well. A good omelette must be served *baveuse* (frothy) and must not be too much cooked.

To make an omelette break six eggs into a bowl, add pepper and salt, and stir with a fork so as to break the yolks and mix them into the whites. *Do not beat up the eggs too long*; add a tiny drop of water. Melt an ounce of butter in a frying-pan, pour in the beaten eggs, and let it cook over a clear fire, carefully detaching the edge of the omelette away from the sides of the pan during the whole process of cooking. Transfer the omelette into a hot dish, roll up the edges, and make it into an oval shape.

To make it frothy, the top of the omelette must hardly be cooked.

This is a plain omelette.

OMELETTE AUX FINES-HERBES.
(Omelette with Herbs.)

When beating up the eggs for an omelette, add in a teaspoonful of finely chopped parsley and chervil.

OMELETTE AU LARD.
(Bacon Omelette.)

Cut some bacon into very small dice, fry brown in some butter; then add them to beaten eggs.

OMELETTE AUX CHAMPIGNONS.
(Mushroom Omelette.)

Cut some mushrooms into thin slices, cook them in a little butter, and place them in the middle of the omelette just before folding it up.

OMELETTE AU ROGNON DE MOUTON.
(Kidney Omelette.)

Slice up a grilled kidney and put it on the top of the omelette just before folding it up.

OMELETTE A L'OSEILLE.
(Sorrel Omelette.)

Put some sorrel (cooked as in the recipe) *œufs durs à l'oseille* into the middle of the omelette before rolling it up.

Note.—Spinach may also be used in the same way.

OMELETTE AUX TOMATES.
(Tomato Omelette.)

Fry some slices of tomato in some butter, and mix into the beaten eggs when making the omelette.

OMELETTE AU FROMAGE.
(Cheese Omelette.)

Stir two large spoonfuls of grated parmesan cheese into the beaten eggs for an omelette.

OMELETTE LYONNAISE.
(Lyonnaise Omelette.)

Cut up some onions and fry them brown in some butter. Stir them into the beaten eggs for an omelette.

Excellent omelettes may be made with any kind of cooked vegetables left over from the day before. Sliced cold potatoes, green peas, French beans, &c., are excellent when re-cooked in an omelette. The heart of a cold artichoke, cut sliced and mixed in with the beaten eggs of an omelette, makes a most excellent breakfast dish.

FONDU AU FROMAGE.
(Cheese Fondu.)

This may be made in a chafing-dish. Take six eggs, a third part of their weight of grated gruyère cheese, and a sixth part of butter, some pepper, and a very little salt. Put all these ingredients into a saucepan or chafing-dish and cook over a moderate fire, stirring meanwhile. The *fondu* must be of the consistency of thick Devonshire cream. Serve on slices of buttered toast in a very hot deep dish.

BEEF.

The beef which has served to make the *pot-au-feu* may be re-dressed in several ways and so regain a certain savour.

The most ordinary way of serving it is with thick tomato or piquante sauce, but there are several other recipes, each of which is excellent.

BŒUF MIROTON.
(Miroton Beef.)

Take about one pound and a half of boiled beef. Cut it into slices about half an inch thick and pare off all pieces of fat and gristle. Cover the bottom of a shallow baking-dish with the slices of beef, and season with pepper and salt.

Cut and prepare one pound of onions, and cook them in butter until they turn a fine golden brown colour. Sprinkle over with flour and a little more salt and pepper, and let them cook for five minutes; then add a wine-glassful of good stock or Bovril, and stir up the whole for twenty minutes over the fire. Add a small spoonful of French mustard, and pour the whole mixture over the slices of beef. Then put it into the oven for twenty minutes, and serve hot.

BŒUF EN SALADE.
(Salad of Boiled Beef.)

Cut one pound and a half of boiled beef into dice about an inch square, paring off all fat and gristle. Put the meat into a salad-bowl with half a wine-glassful of cold stock, two spoonfuls of vinegar, and salt and pepper. Let it soak for two hours, then add four spoonfuls of oil and chopped onion or shallot to taste. Mix thoroughly, and serve.

BŒUF AU GRATIN.
(Boiled Beef au gratin.)

Cut the beef as for a *miroton*, add a wine-glassful of stock, salt and pepper to taste, and sprinkle over with fine bread crumbs. Brown in a quick oven for a quarter of an hour.

BOULETTES OU RISSOLES DE BŒUF.
(Rissoles of Beef.)

Mince some pieces of boiled beef and mix with soft bread crumbs previously soaked in milk. Add pepper, salt, a taste of shallot, and dried herbs. Make into balls; roll the balls in flour or fine bread crumbs and fry in butter. Rissoles are specially good when served with tomato sauce.

BŒUF SAUCE PIQUANTE.
(Beef with Sauce Piquante.)

Slice some cold boiled beef and warm up the slices

for fifteen minutes in some *sauce piquante* (see Sauces), allowing them to simmer but not to boil.

BŒUF MODE.
(Beef à la Mode.)

Take a thick piece of rump of beef about two pounds in weight; lard it with strips of fat bacon about a third of an inch thick. Tie up the piece of meat with string so as to make it as compact as possible. Put it into an earthen pan or pipkin, with a small wine-glassful of white wine, a tumblerful of water, two unboned calves' feet, previously boiled for some minutes, and the rind of the bacon, salt and pepper to taste. Let it boil up, and skim it as for *pot-au-feu*. Then add one pound of small carrots, one or two onions, three or four cloves, a bunch of herbs, and more pepper and salt. Let it simmer gently for four hours on the side of the fire. Then strain the gravy through a colander and place the meat, vegetables, and calves' feet on a dish. Pour the gravy over it and serve. Some people add a taste of garlic.

BŒUF-MODE FROID.
(Same Dish—Cold.)

Served cold in a deep dish, the gravy becomes a thick jelly. Cold *bœuf-mode* is an excellent dish for luncheon.

BIFTECK AU BEURRE D'ANCHOIS.

(Anchovy Butter with Steak.)

Take an anchovy and press and crush it with a knife on the table. Mix it into two ounces of butter, press through a sieve, then place it upon a small piece of grilled beefsteak sufficient for one person.

FILET-DE-BŒUF.

The finest piece of roast beef served upon French tables is the fillet, which is known in England as the undercut in the sirloin. This portion of the animal is served as an entrée upon a bed of vegetables, which vary according to the season, or garnished with various sauces, &c. The following recipes are all composed of roasted fillet together with some *garniture* or dressing:—

FILET AUX CHAMPIGNONS.

(Fillet with Mushrooms.)

Cook a fine piece of fillet in butter, in a small pan over the fire. Take out the meat and add a little flour to the butter in which fillet has cooked, and stir up well with a wooden spoon. Pepper and salt to taste. Add the liquor in which some mushrooms have cooked and a little stock. Pass through a sieve. Then add the mushrooms and serve the fillet with the mushrooms around it. Pour the sauce over the whole and serve.

FILET AUX OLIVES.
(Fillet with Olives.)

Same as above, substituting olives for mushrooms.

FILET À LA FINANCIÈRE.
(Fillet à la Financière.)

This *garniture* is composed of forcemeat balls, mushrooms, truffles, cockscombs, &c., mixed with a *béchamel sauce grasse.* (See Sauces, p. 14.)

FILET À L'ALLEMANDE.
(Fillet à l'Allemande.)

The roasted fillet is served upon a bed of cabbages previously parboiled and then stewed in stock and mixed with butter.

FILET À LA JARDINIÈRE.
(Fillet à la Jardinière.)

The roasted fillet is served upon a bed of mixed vegetables. (See Macedoine, p. 164.)

FILET À LA BORDELAISE.
(Fillet à la Bordelaise.)

The *bordelaise* is a mixture of cèpes or mushrooms cut into fine slices, sliced tomatoes, chopped garlic, and sweet herbs, mixed together with *béchamel sauce grasse* (see Sauces, p. 14), and is used as a *garniture* around the roasted fillet.

FILET À L'ITALIENNE.
(Fillet à l'Italienne.)

The *garniture* is composed of Italian pastes, such as macaroni, *lazangnes*, or *nouilles*, previously boiled and mixed with rich gravy or stock, and a sprinkling of grated parmesan if desired.

FILET À LA PORTUGAISE.
(Fillet à la Portugaise.)

The garniture is composed of sliced tomatoes, sliced sour oranges, and sliced onions, mixed together and stewed in stock. A *béchamel grasse* (see Sauces) may be added if desired, and greatly improves the garniture.

FILET À LA PROVENÇALE.
(Fillet à la Provençale.)

This *garniture* is composed of the sliced hearts of parboiled artichokes, egg-plants, and tomatoes. These are stewed together in stock or *béchamel grasse*. (See Sauces.)

FILET À LA CRÉOLE.
(Fillet à la Créole.)

The roasted fillet is served with curried rice.

FILET À LA PRINTANIÈRE.
(Fillet à la Printanière.)

Green peas and French beans mixed together with *béchamel grasse* (see Sauces) compose this *garniture*.

FILET SAUCE MADÈRE.

(Fillet à la Sauce Madère.)

Make a *roux* and stir in a wine-glassful or tumblerful of good Madeira wine. Serve hot with the roasted fillet.

FILET À LA PURÉE DE LÉGUMES.

(Fillet à la purée de légumes.)

The roasted fillet is served upon a bed of *purée* of any vegetables, such as potatoes, endives, carrots, turnips, &c.

TRANCHES DE FILET RÔTI AU CÉLERI.

(Slice of Roast Fillet or Sirloin of Beef with Celery.)

Choose some fine celery and clean it, then cook in good stock. When cooked, add some very thin slices from a roasted fillet or sirloin of beef, with chopped shallots, and lemon juice. This dish may be made with chicory, cucumbers, &c.

TRANCHES DE FILET DE BŒUF SAUTÉ.

(Slices of Fillet of Beef Stewed.)

Cut some slices off a fillet of beef, put them into a stewpan over a quick fire, with a little butter. Keep turning them till they begin to brown, then lift them from the pan; add some brown sauce made separately, moisten with a little good broth and a wine-glassful of white wine. Season with salt, pepper, and chopped parsley. Put back the meat into this sauce for a few moments, then serve. (For brown sauce, see recipe on page 12.)

CULOTTE DE BŒUF BRAISÉ À LA PURÉE DE TOMATES.

(Braised Rump of Beef with Tomato Sauce.)

Tie up about two pounds or two pounds and a half of rump of beef, put it in a pan with half a bottle of white wine, a little brandy, a quart of broth, a few onions, three cloves, a few carrots, a bunch of herbs and parsley, some salt, and a few peppercorns. Simmer for ten or twelve minutes, skim, then finally cook in an oven, taking care to check it every half-hour.

The piece of beef being cooked, it is taken out of its gravy, to which some thick tomato sauce is added. This mixture is cooked for two minutes over the fire and is poured over the meat, which is then served up.

NOIX-DE-BŒUF À LA GELÉE.

(Glazed Round of Beef.)

This portion of beef being dry, care must be taken that it is well covered with fat. Lard it with thick strips of bacon; put it in an earthen pot with carrots, onions, a bunch of herbs, pepper and sweet spices, moisten with white wine and a glassful of brandy; cover and cook slowly. When the stew is finished, strain carefully, then put it back to simmer down a little. Serve in its own sauce.

LANGUE DE BŒUF BRAISÉE.
(Braised Ox Tongue.)

After having washed and trimmed the tongue, lard it with bacon cut into dice. Cook it slowly in a saucepan for four or five hours, adding slices of bacon, veal or beef, carrots, onions, thyme, laurel, and cloves. When ready to serve, skim it, cut it down the middle, and serve with piquante sauce.

LANGUE DE BŒUF AU GRATIN.
(Ox tongue au gratin.)

Cook the tongue over a wood fire, then remove the skin; let it get cold and cut into slices. Hash with parsley, shallots, a little tarragon, some capers, and an anchovy; soak some bread crumbs in broth, put all in a mortar and pound, adding meanwhile a little butter. After this is done, put it on a dish; pour over it some melted butter and broth; place the dish in a slow oven, and when browned it is ready to serve.

LANGUE DE BŒUF EN PAPILLOTES.
(Ox Tongue en papillote.)

After the tongue is cooked, cut it into even slices, cover with sweet herbs and a slice of bacon, then envelop each piece in a greased paper, folding it tightly so that the gravy cannot escape. Put on the grille for a few minutes, and serve.

LANGUE DE BŒUF EN SAUCE PIQUANTE.

(Ox Tongue à la Sauce Piquante.)

Stew the ox tongue in some weak stock. When cooked remove the skin and serve with *piquante sauce*, or *ravigote*, or *Robert* sauce. (See Sauces.)

LANGUE DE BŒUF À LA CHOUCROUTE.

(Ox Tongue with Sauerkraut.)

The ox tongue must remain for ten or twelve days in salt. Then soak in fresh water for two hours and cook slowly for two hours or until the skin is easily removable in water. When done remove the skin, and serve on a *garniture* of sauerkraut. (See Choucroute, p. 157.)

LANGUE DE BŒUF À LA PURÉE DE POMMES DE TERRE.

(Ox Tongue and Mashed Potatoes.)

Serve the ox tongue on a bed of mashed potatoes. (See *Pommes de Terre en Purée*, p. 131.)

ROGNON DE BŒUF SAUTÉ.

(Fried Beef Kidney.)

Cut into small pieces an ox kidney, being careful to remove all grease. Cook the pieces in butter, and as soon as they are browned, flour them, cook them a little more, and moisten with broth and red wine, adding shallots and thickly chopped parsley. Serve quickly.

CERVELLE DE BŒUF AU BEURRE-NOIR.

(Ox Brains with Black Butter.)

Pare and trim some ox brains; soak for an hour in slightly warmed water with a few drops of vinegar. Strain off and cook in salted water for thirty minutes. Serve with *sauce au beurre noir*. (See Sauces, p. 13.)

CERVELLE À LA MAÎTRE D'HÔTEL.

(Ox Brains à la Maître d'Hôtel.)

Prepare the brains. Fry in butter, and serve with *maître d'hôtel* sauce. (See Sauces.)

CERVELLE À LA MAYONNAISE.

(Ox Brains à la Printànière.)

Cut each brain into four pieces; roll lightly in flour and fry for fifteen minutes in butter. Serve with *mayonnaise* or *remoulade* sauce in a sauce-boat. (See Sauces.)

CERVELLE À LA PRINTANIÈRE.

(Ox Brains à la Printànière.)

Prepare as in preceding recipe, and serve with a *purée* of tomatoes, or sorrel, or spinach, or lettuce. (See Vegetables.)

FOIE DE BŒUF AUX CAROTTES AND AUX OIGNONS.

(Liver of Beef with Carrots and Onions.)

Lard a pound and a half of ox's liver with thick *lardons* of fat bacon. Put it into a saucepan with some butter. When slightly browned, stir in a little flour. Add eight or ten carrots and as many onions, salt and pepper, and two tumblerfuls of stock, water, or wine. Let it simmer for two hours, then serve on a deep dish in its own gravy. Garnish with the carrots and onions.

VEAL.

TÊTE DE VEAU SAUCE PAUVRE HOMME.
(Calf's Head à la Sauce Pauvre Homme.)

Bone a calf's head, take out the brain, and after having divested it of the red skin which binds it, put it to soak for an hour. Then cook it apart in acidulated water and leave it in its liquor until it is time to serve. Boil the head, take out the tongue, and remove the inferior parts. Then let it cool, and cut it into four pieces. Put them into a large saucepan. In another saucepan put one pound of chopped beef suet, a bunch of sweet herbs, some onions and carrots cut into rings, a little flour, four quarts of water, salt, peppercorns, and a liqueur glass of vinegar. When this mixture is boiling, pour it into the saucepan with the pieces of calf's head, adding the tongue. Let the whole cook for two hours and a half; take the pieces out of the saucepan, strain them, and serve on a folded serviette in an oval dish.

TÊTE DE VEAU EN TORTUE.
(Calf's Head en Tortue.)

Boil and bone a small calf's head. Soak the brain apart in a pan of cold water. Cut off the two ears, and cut up the rest of the head into pieces about two and a half inches square. Put the pieces with the ears, the tongue, and all the bones into an enamelled saucepan with two quarts of water, a pint of white wine, half a tumblerful of vinegar, and two large spoonfuls of flour mixed with a little cold water. Let the meat simmer over a moderate fire for two hours. Skim carefully; then take out the bones and add the brains. Cook for another half-hour. When the pieces are quite soft, reduce the liquor to a quart and a half. With this liquor make a *roux;* add a pinch of cayenne pepper, a spoonful of French mustard, and three spoonfuls of thick gravy. Let this sauce reduce, and when it has thickened put in the tongue, skinned and cut into pieces, as well as the other portions of the head. Let these ingredients simmer together for another half-hour, and serve on a very deep dish, pouring the sauce over the meat, and serving the brain on the top between the ears. Garnish with a *garniture* composed of twenty-five or thirty stoned olives, ten pickled gherkins cut into strips, twenty-five mushrooms fried in butter, eight quartered hard-boiled eggs, eight or ten truffles, four or five cockscombs, and five or six crayfish.

Note.—While the pieces of tongue and head are simmering together, the ears and brain must be kept warm together in a little sauce in another saucepan.

POITRÍNE DE VEAU AUX PETITS-POIS.
(Breast of Veal with Green Peas.)

Cut a part of the breast into pieces and boil them.

Strain off and cook them in butter; stir in some flour, adding stock, a bunch of sweet herbs, and pepper. In another saucepan cook some green peas; add a little sugar and the yolks of two eggs. Serve up over the veal.

BLANQUETTE DE VEAU.
(Blanquette of Veal.)

This can be made with fresh breast of veal or of the lean remains of roast veal. Cut the meat into thin slices, make a white butter sauce, moisten it with broth, let it thicken and warm the veal with it. Bind the sauce with the yolks of eggs and a little fresh butter, adding to it a little lemon juice, some chopped shallots and parsley, and serve up the slices of meat in it.

POITRINE DE VEAU AU BLANC.
(Breast of Veal au Blanc.)

Lay some strips of bacon at the bottom of a saucepan, take about a pound and a half of breast of veal previously trimmed and parboiled and place it on the bacon, sprinkle with flour; add a bunch of herbs, a few carrots, onions, and some slices of lemon. Pour about three tumblerfuls of stock or water over it, and let it cook on a moderate fire. Before serving bind the sauce with the yolks of two eggs.

FOIE DE VEAU SAUTÉ.
(Fried Calf's Liver.)

Cut the liver in three slices, season with salt and pepper, and dredge with flour. Melt a piece of butter in a frying-pan, put in the slices of liver; cook on both sides; take them out and keep them hot. To the butter which remains in the pan, add flour, shallots, parsley, mushrooms finely chopped, and pour over equal quantities of stock and white wine. Let the sauce thicken; put back the slices of liver for a few minutes into the sauce. Then serve, pouring the sauce over the liver.

FOIE DE VEAU BRAISÉ À L'ITALIENNE.
(Calf's Liver Braised à l'Italienne.)

Cut the liver into thin slices. In a saucepan put a little refined olive oil, some dice of bacon, white wine, chopped parsley, and spring onions and mushrooms seasoned with salt and pepper. On this lay the slices of liver. Over the liver place another layer of the same ingredients, then a layer of liver, and so on. Cover the whole with strips of fat bacon, and let it cook on a slow fire. Serve with *sauce Italienne* (see Sauces, p. 15) or with its own gravy reduced and skimmed.

FOIE DE VEAU SAUTÉ À L'ITALIENNE.

Cut the liver into slices, season with salt and pepper and dredge with flour. Put it into a frying-pan with some butter; brown it on both sides; do not leave it in the pan for more than five minutes. Take it out, and into the butter stir three or four ounces of very finely chopped onion. Cook for five minutes, and serve over the slices of liver. Garnish with slices of lemon.

FOIE DE VEAU À LA BOURGEOISE.
(Calf's Liver à la Bourgeoise.)

Lard two pounds of calf's liver with strips of fat bacon. Put the meat into a saucepan with a quarter pound of butter, and let it brown on all sides. Then take out the liver and mix two ounces of flour into the butter, and stir for five minutes. Then add two pints of water, two pints of white wine, a bunch of parsley, one onion stuck with two cloves, salt and pepper. Stir until it boils; then put back the meat and add twenty pieces of carrots cut into the shape of a cork. Cover over the pan, leaving a small aperture, and let it simmer on a slow fire. After the dish has cooked for two hours, add ten onions previously browned in butter. Leave the meat on the fire for another hour. Strain the sauce through a sieve and serve. Garnish with the carrots and onions.

LANGUE DE VEAU À L'ÉTUVÉE.
(Calf's Tongue à l'étuvée.)

Parboil the calf's tongue, and lard it with thin strips of fat bacon; season with spice and sweet herbs; place it in a saucepan with two carrots, two onions, and three cloves, pouring over some stock, and let it cook slowly for four hours. Take it off the fire, skim it, and serve with *piquante sauce* (see Sauces, p. 15), *ravigote*, or *poivrade*.

PIED DE VEAU À LA POULETTE.
(Calf's Foot à la Poulette.)

Bone, boil, and cut into pieces some calves' feet. Place them in a saucepan with butter; dredge with flour, and pour over them stock or water. Add pepper, salt, a bunch of sweet herbs, some small mushrooms, and onions. When cooked, bind the sauce with yolks of eggs and a few drops of vinegar.

SWEETBREADS.

To prepare sweetbreads for cooking they must first be soaked and thoroughly washed in fresh water; then boil for a quarter of an hour in salted boiling water.

RIS DE VEAU À LA POULETTE.
(Sweetbreads à la Poulette.)

Take some sweetbreads, boil and strain them, place them in a saucepan with a piece of butter; dredge with flour; stir in a little water; add salt and pepper and a bunch of parsley. Cook slowly, and when serving, add small onions and mushrooms cooked apart. Bind the sauce with yolks of eggs and a few drops of vinegar.

RIS DE VEAU À L'OSEILLE.
(Sweetbreads with Sorrel.)

Put a large piece of fresh butter into an earthen pan, and let it cook until it clarifies. Put in the pieces of parboiled sweetbreads, turning them from time to time; add a little stock and let the sweetbreads cook until they are browned and slightly glazed. Serve on a *purée* of sorrel. (See Purée d'Oseille, p. 137.)

RIS DE VEAU À LA FINANCIÈRE.
(Sweetbreads à la Financière.)

Prepare the sweetbreads as in preceding recipe, then warm them up in a sauce composed of small mushrooms, stoned olives, two sliced truffles, and a *béchamel grasse* sauce (see Sauces) or some rich gravy.

RIS DE VEAU À LA ROMAINE.
(Sweetbreads à la Romaine.)

Prepare and parboil some sweetbreads. Make a *béchamel grasse* (see Sauces), and to it add some small mushrooms and some stoned olives, together with the pieces of sweetbread. Serve in a deep dish, garnished with macaroni or *nouilles* previously boiled and mixed with butter.

RIS DE VEAU EN FRICANDEAU.
(Sweetbreads en fricandeau.)

Take some sweetbreads, remove the inferior parts

and parboil them. Lard with very good bacon and season. Cook over a good wood fire for three-quarters of an hour. Take them off the fire, and let the sauce thicken. Add a little sifted sugar, put back the sweetbreads for a few moments, and serve the whole on a *purée* of sorrel or tomatoes, chestnuts or mushrooms, spinach or cooked endive.

RIS DE VEAU EN PAPILLOTES.
(Sweetbreads en papillotes.)

Parboil the sweetbreads and cook them over a good fire, strain off and put them on a dish. Pour over some good *duxelles* sauce (see Sauces, p. 14), and let the whole cool. Cut some thin slices of ham, sandwich each sweetbread, well saturated with sauce, between two slices of ham, oil some white sheets of paper, wrap the sandwich carefully in them; put into the oven, and when the paper browns, serve.

TRIPES À LA MODE DE CAEN.
(Tripe à la Mode de Caen.)

Take two pounds of tripe, clean it well, and cut it into strips about three inches long. Throw the strips into water and let them boil five minutes. Then cut a pound of bacon into small dice about an inch thick, bone a calf's foot, and cut it into six pieces. Put all the ingredients together into a large saucepan; then add one quart of good stock, a quarter of a pound of onions, a bunch of herbs, salt and pepper to taste. Cover over the saucepan and let it come to boiling point. Then put it on the side of the fire and let it simmer gently for three hours. Before serving the dish, take out the onions and the bunch of herbs. Serve in a vegetable dish with a cover.

PETITES CÔTELETTES DE VEAU, OU ESCALOPES DE VEAU À LA MILANAISE.

(Scallop or Cutlet of Veal à la Milanaise.)

Take some trimmed cutlets or one or two fine veal scallops, roll them in flour and fry in olive oil. Strain them off and serve with slices of lemon.

NOIX DE VEAU EN GELÉE.

(Round of Veal en Gelée.)

Take three pounds of round or haunch of veal, bone it and tie it up with fine string, and brown it in a mixture of dripping and butter over a slow fire. When it is well browned, take it out of the saucepan and put it aside. Put into the saucepan one large calf's foot with the bones and trimmings of the meat. Add two large tumblerfuls of white wine, a liqueur glassful of brandy, two quarts of water, a few carrots, onions, a bunch of herbs, &c. Boil up these ingredients on a quick fire, then skim and moderate the cooking as for *pot-au-feu*. After three hours' cooking the calf's foot and bones will be quite cooked; add the piece of veal, let it boil up and then simmer

French Dishes for English Tables.

slowly for three more hours. Great care must be taken not to crush the carrots when the meat is put in. When done, the meat is put into a bowl or mould. Pieces of carrots and French beans, slices of truffles, green peas, &c., are placed around the meat, and the sauce is passed through a fine sieve and allowed to cool for two hours in an earthen pan before it is poured over the meat. The jelly must set for twelve hours in a cool place. Before serving, the fat which has risen to the surface must be removed. Then take out the contents of the mould and serve on a dish.

MUTTON.

GIGOT-CHEVREUIL.

(Leg of Mutton served as Venison.)

Take a small leg of mutton, weighing about five pounds, and soak it in the following pickle for two days in the summer or three or four days in the winter:—

One quart of water, one quart of white wine, two tumblerfuls of white vinegar, four or five carrots, two bay leaves, four or five onions, a sprig of thyme, a bunch of parsley, salt, and peppercorns.

This mixture must be put into an earthenware pan or *terrine*, and the leg of mutton must be turned twice a day.

Before roasting the meat, it must be carefully wrapped in thick buttered paper.

Baste with a portion of the pickle.

GIGOT DE MOUTON BRAISÉ.

(Braised Leg of Mutton.)

Bone a leg of mutton, lard it with thick strips of fat bacon. Brown it for twenty minutes in a half-covered saucepan in two ounces of butter and the same quantity of lard or dripping; season with spice, salt and pepper, chopped parsley, and spring onions.

French Dishes for English Tables. 79

Put six carrots and as many onions into a covered pan, and lay in the meat. Pour in some good stock and half a glassful of brandy. Add thyme, three bay leaves, three cloves, and a little garlic, and a boned calf's foot, cover with the lid; let it cook slowly in an oven for five hours. Then take out the leg of mutton, and serve in its own gravy or on endives boiled and mashed.

EPAULE DE MOUTON EN BALLON.

Bone a shoulder of mutton and lard it, tie it with string in the shape of a ball, and braise it like a leg of mutton.

CARBONADE DE MOUTON.
(Carbonade of Mutton.)

This is a recipe from Provence.

Separate the bones in a fillet of mutton, but do not take them out of the meat. Tie up tightly with fine string. Lay on a bed made of strips of bacon, two or three carrots and some trimmings of knuckle bone of veal, and put into a braising-pan. Lay in the mutton, and pour over it a tumblerful of stock and two large spoonfuls of brandy. Cover with a thick sheet of buttered paper under the lid of the saucepan. Cook for four hours without touching the meat. Half an hour before serving, simmer the gravy, and serve with a *sauce piquante* or a *purée* of *champignons* prepared in the following manner:—
Remove the stalks of the mushrooms and boil until

quite tender. Chop up finely and stew in stock and *roux*. Crush with a fork and stir till boiling point. Serve.

GIGOT DE SEPT HEURES.
(Leg of Mutton de Sept Heures.)

This is a very old-fashioned recipe, and is prepared like a braised leg of mutton without the calves' feet. Let the meat cook over a slow fire for seven hours, adding a little white wine and tomato sauce from time to time.

Like the fillet of beef, the leg of mutton is the choicest piece of the animal, and may be served roasted, with several different *garnitures* to form an entrée.

The following recipes are the best:—

GIGOT AUX HARICOTS.
(Leg of Mutton with White Beans.)

Roast the leg of mutton, and serve with haricot beans (see recipes) mixed with rich gravy.

A purée of *haricots*, or *flageolets*, or *marrons* is excellent as a *garniture*.

GIGOT AUX CHAMPIGNONS.
(Leg of Mutton with Mushrooms.)

Fry some mushrooms or *cèpes* in butter or dripping. Mix with rich gravy and serve around the roast leg of mutton.

GIGOT AUX LENTILLES.
(Leg of Mutton with Lentils.)

The lentils are served plain or *en purée* and mixed with gravy around the meat.

GIGOT À LA FINANCIÈRE.
(Leg of Mutton à la Financière.)

(See recipe Filet à la Financière.)

GIGOT À LA MILANAISE.
(Leg of Mutton à la Milanaise.)

Parboil some macaroni, then let it simmer for half an hour in some mixture of gravy, butter, and tomato sauce. Serve the leg of mutton on a thick layer of the macaroni.

GIGOT AUX CAROTTES.
(Leg of Mutton with Carrots.)

Parboil some young round carrots; then fry them in butter with chopped parsley. Serve the leg of mutton with a garniture of the carrots.

GIGOT À LA JARDINIÈRE.
(Leg of Mutton Jardinière.)

(See Filet de Bœuf Jardinière.)

GIGOT AUX TOMATES.
(Leg of Mutton with Tomatoes.)

The tomatoes may be served with mutton in three

ways:—Either forced whole and placed around the meat, or sliced and fried, or *en purée*. (See recipes.)

GIGOT AUX CŒURS DE LAITUES.
(Leg of Mutton with Stewed Lettuce.)

Parboil the hearts of some fine young lettuces. Strain them off, and stew them for ten minutes in butter thickened with a very little flour. Pour over some rich gravy and serve around the meat.

GIGOT AUX CŒURS D'ARTICHAUTS.
(Leg of Mutton with Hearts of Artichokes.)

Parboil the hearts of some artichokes; strain them off and cook in butter for ten minutes, without allowing them to brown. When quite tender, pour over a little weak stock. Serve around the meat.

CÔTELETTES DE MOUTON À LA JARDINIÈRE.
(Mutton Cutlets à la Jardinière.)

Trim the cutlets and lard them with thin strips of fat bacon; place them in a saucepan on some thin slices of ham previously warmed up. Season with pepper, salt, and parsley, and pour over some good stock. Serve on a dish of mashed vegetables, then skim the gravy and pour it over the meat.

CERVELLES DE MOUTON FRITES.
(Fried Sheep's Brains.)

Take some sheep's brains, wash well in cold water,

and separate into small pieces, carefully removing the small filaments. Make a paste with three tablespoonfuls of flour, three eggs, a glassful of milk, and a glassful of water; mix thoroughly. Dip the pieces of brain into this mixture, and fry in boiling lard.

CERVELLES AU GRATIN.
(Sheep's Brains au gratin.)

Boil some rice in some weak stock. When nearly cooked, mix in some gravy. Line the bottom of a deep baking dish with the rice, lay in the pieces of parboiled brain, some slices of parboiled eggs, and dredge with grated parmesan cheese. Put another layer of rice over these ingredients, and dredge with parmesan. Add sufficient butter, and brown in the oven. The rice must be very wet so as not to dry in the oven.

CERVELLES À LA MAYONNAISE.
(Sheep's Brains à la Mayonnaise.)

Soak some sheep's brains in water for fifteen minutes; then boil for another fifteen minutes in salted water. Remove the skin and filaments, and roll the pieces of brain in flour. Fry in butter, and serve garnished with slices of lemon and a good mayonnaise served in a sauce-boat.

CERVELLES EN BLANQUETTE.
(Sheep's Brains en Blanquette.)

Make a blanquette (see recipe, Blanquette de Veau,

p. 70) and lay in the pieces of brain previously boiled with boiled mushrooms, &c.

HARICOT-DE-MOUTON.
(Haricot of Mutton.)

Take two pounds of breast of mutton or of the shoulder, cut into pieces about three inches square. Put three ounces of butter into a saucepan with salt and pepper, and let the meat cook in it for a quarter of an hour, taking care that the butter does not burn and that each piece of meat lies separately in the pan. Then dredge with flour and let it brown. Add a quart of water, and stir with a wooden spoon till it boils. Then let it simmer for one hour, adding a bunch of herbs, one onion, and two cloves. Meanwhile, take one pound of turnips, carefully peeled, and ten small onions and fry them in a pan with some butter. Add these to the meat, when they have cooked for an hour. About twenty minutes later add one dozen potatoes about the size of a pigeon's egg. Let this dish cook for two hours and a half. Before serving, take out the bunch of herbs and cloves and skim the sauce.

PIEDS DE MOUTON À LA POULETTE.
(Sheep's Trotters à la Poulette.)

Throw the trotters into boiling water, take them out, cut them lengthwise, and take out the big bone. Wipe, and cook them in white sauce for five hours. Melt some butter, and before it becomes brown stir in some flour. Add some stock, a bunch of parsley, two onions, some cloves, a bay leaf, and a few small mushrooms. Let this mixture cook for one hour and a half. Then put in the trotters. Before serving, bind with a small piece of butter, the yolk of an egg, and a few drops of lemon juice. This sauce must be as thick as fresh cream.

PIEDS DE MOUTON À LA LYONNAISE.
(Sheep's Trotters à la Lyonnaise.)

Prepare as in the preceding recipe, and cut the feet into pieces. Put some butter into a saucepan with finely sliced onions, mix in a little flour, and when brown, add some stock. Boil down for ten minutes, and before serving, warm up the pieces of trotter in the mixture.

PIEDS DE MOUTON SAUCE ROBERT.
(Sheep's Trotters à la Sauce Robert.)

Prepare as for trotters *à la Poulette*, then put them into a sauce *Robert*. Let them simmer for a few minutes, and serve.

GOULACHE.
(Mutton Goulache.)

Take some small chops, or boned shoulder of mutton, cut into small squares about two inches thick. Cut up some onions and fry in butter, stir in a little flour, add the meat, pepper, and salt. When the meat has browned, add a pound of sliced tomatoes, from which the pips and cores have been removed. Add half a teaspoonful of red *paprica* (Hungarian red pepper made of crushed chilis). Add a glassful of stock or water; cover the saucepan, and let the meat simmer for three hours. Parboil some fine pearl barley, and add it to the meat with rather more than a cupful of water to each table-spoonful of barley. Cook for one hour, stirring from time to time, so that the barley does not stick. Serve in a deep dish.

Note.—Curry powder may be substituted for *paprica*.

LAMB.

QUARTIER D'AGNEAU À LA BERNOISE.
(Fore-quarter of Lamb à la Bernoise.)

Soak the meat thoroughly in warm melted butter, and roll it in fine bread crumbs. Wrap it up in white buttered paper, and bake in the oven. Serve with slices of lemon.

QUARTIER D'AGNEAU FARCI.
(Fore-quarter of Lamb stuffed.)

Bone a fore-quarter of lamb. Flatten out the meat—the skin underneath. Place in the middle of the meat some good sausage-meat stuffing mixed with a few stoned olives or some sliced truffles. Roll up the lamb and fasten with fine string. Cook—basting with butter from time to time—in a moderate oven for two hours.

CÔTELETTES D'AGNEAU À L'ITALIENNE.
(Lamb Cutlets à l'Italienne.)

Butter some cutlets, dip them into fine bread crumbs, and then into the beaten yolk of an egg.

Fry them in boiling fat or butter, and serve with lemon.

CÔTELETTES D'AGNEAU AUX LEGUMES FRAIS.

(Lamb Cutlets and Fresh Vegetables.)

Fry the cutlets and serve with cardoons, hearts of artichokes or mushrooms fried in butter or stewed in stock. (See recipes.)

CÔTELETTES EN DEMI-DEUIL.

(Cutlets in Half-mourning.)

Mix some white mushrooms and sliced truffles in a rich gravy sauce. Cook until tender, and serve under fried cutlets.

BLANQUETTE D'AGNEAU.

(Blanquette of Lamb.)

(See recipe for Blanquette de Veau, p. 70.)

To the Blanquette d'Agneau a few stoned olives and parboiled mushrooms may be added as a great improvement.

POULTRY.

DINDE EN DAUBE.
(Turkey en daube.)

Prepare a turkey, put it into a saucepan on a bed made of strips of fat bacon, sweet herbs, onions, carrots, thyme, bay leaf, salt and pepper, nutmeg and spices. Cover the turkey in the same manner, so that the air is entirely excluded. Cover the pan tightly, and let it cook from three to four hours. Take it out, strain the liquor through a fine sieve, and serve, pouring the gravy over the turkey. This dish may be served cold when the gravy has become a thick jelly.

COLD ROAST TURKEY SAUCE ROBERT.

Prick with a fork the remains of a cold roast turkey, salt and pepper to taste, grill over a slow fire, and serve with sauce *Robert*.

CAPILOTADE DE DINDE.
(Capilotade of Turkey.)

Cut up the pieces of cold roast turkey and place them in an Italian sauce (see page 15). Let them boil a few moments and serve, pouring the sauce over the meat. Garnish with sippets.

ABATIS DE DINDE.
(Giblets.)

Take the giblets of a good turkey, the liver, and the gizzard; singe the wings, the head, and the neck, and crush the legs. Clean the gizzard and cut it into four. Do not use the head, which gives a bad taste to the dish. Put two ounces of butter in a saucepan, throw in the giblets with the liver and gizzard. Cut up a quarter of a pound of fat bacon into four pieces, and let it brown with the giblets, then take out all the ingredients except the butter, stir in a large spoonful of flour and let it brown. Then add two glasses of water, pepper, salt, thyme, a bay leaf, and one onion stuck over with cloves. Put back the giblets and bacon into this mixture, and let the whole cook for two hours. Meanwhile boil a dozen turnips, adding slices of carrots, a few potatoes, and one head of celery, for a quarter of an hour in boiling water, strain off. Put the vegetables into the pot with the giblets and a piece of sugar about the size of a small walnut. When cooked, skim, and serve very hot.

ABATIS DE DINDE À LA CHIPOLATA.
(Giblets à la Chipolata.)

Scald and singe some turkey giblets, cut the necks into four pieces, the wings and legs into two, and the gizzard into four. Only use the liver, which must be very fresh. Cut some lean bacon into large dice and brown them in some fresh butter, with some turnips cut into the shape of a large walnut, some parboiled carrots cut into the same shape, and onions into rings. Take out the bacon and vegetables and put them on a dish. Then fry the giblets to a deep brown, and mix a spoonful of flour into the butter. Stir for five minutes on the fire, and add equal quantities of stock and water and two large tablespoonfuls of brandy. Stir until boiling point, then let it simmer down. Add the bacon and carrots and a bunch of parsley. Half an hour before serving add the onions and turnips, some chipolata sausages, and a few good grilled chestnuts. Let it simmer for another ten minutes, skim, and serve.

POULE-AU-POT.

(Fowl in the Pot.)

The fowl is boiled in the *pot-au-feu* with the usual quantities of meat and vegetables. When the pot-au-feu is finished, take out the fowl, sprinkle with salt, and serve.

POULE AUX OIGNONS.

(Fowl with Onions.)

Cut some bacon into small pieces and fry in butter. Take them out and put them on a plate. Into the same saucepan put the fowl, adding butter if necessary. When thoroughly browned, take it out,

mix some flour into the butter, and add some stock.
Put back the fowl and bacon into the mixture for a
few minutes, and serve.

POULE-AU-RIZ.
(Fowl with Rice.)

Truss the fowl with the feet inwards, tie around
it a thin strip of fat bacon. Boil about three-quarters
of a pound of fine rice, strain it off, and put it into
a saucepan with the fowl placed breast downwards.
Add some stock, cover the saucepan and let it cook
slowly, stirring from time to time. When the fowl
is cooked put it on a dish, stir a piece of fresh butter
into the rice, salt and pepper, and serve around the
fowl.

POULET SAUTÉ.
(Sauté Fowl.)

Cut up the fowl as for a fricassée, put it into a
saucepan with butter; stir in a little flour, and add
equal quantities of stock and white wine, salt and
pepper, chopped parsley and mushrooms. When it
boils let it boil down again for fifteen minutes, skim
the sauce, and serve.

POULARDE À LA GODARD.
(Fowl à la Godard.)

Truss a fowl and put it into a deep saucepan with
some butter; cover it with strips of bacon, and let
it cook without browning. When the liquid it has

thrown off has boiled down, add a few spoonfuls of stock and of tomato sauce (see Sauces), cover, and let it stew with the lid of the pan carefully closed. Towards the end let the bird brown, then take it out and keep it hot. Into the saucepan pour a pint of good stock, mix it with the gravy which remains in the pan, add two glassfuls of champagne, pass through a sieve, put it back into the pan with the bird, add eight or ten cockscombs and as many truffles, forcemeat balls, and pieces of sweetbread. Let the whole simmer together. Serve with triangular-shaped sippets and the hearts of artichokes stewed in stock.

POULARDE À LA MONTMORENCY.
(Fowl à la Montmorency.)

Put a large piece of butter and two tumblerfuls of stock into a saucepan; put in the fowl, but do not let it brown. A few veal trimmings may be added. Baste the bird from time to time with stock, never allowing it to brown. When cooked, take it out and cut it into large pieces; keep them hot. Pound the trimmings of the bird and the pieces of veal in a mortar; mix this with the liquor in which the bird has cooked, and strain through a sieve. In another saucepan melt a large spoonful of fresh butter, mix in some flour, but do not let it brown, add the liquor which has been strained through the sieve, bind with two spoonfuls of cream, and keep it hot in the *bain-marie*, together with the pieces of fowl.

Before serving, add a *garniture* of cockscombs, sliced truffles, small mushrooms, and sliced kidneys. Garnish with crayfish.

POULARDE FARCIE À LA GELÉE.
(Stuffed Fowl in Jelly.)

Bone the back and the stomach of the bird, and stuff it with small slices of veal and ham, the veal predominating. Add a few sliced truffles, and fill in the interstices with forcemeat. Sew up the skin of the back; tie up the bird with fine string, and wrap it in a piece of soft white muslin; put it into a large braising-pan with two parboiled calf's feet and a pound of knuckle of veal previously browned in butter; add salt, peppercorns, and cloves, and pour in some white wine and water, so that the liquid rises about two inches above the bird. Let it boil up, then skim and moderate the fire. Cook slowly for two hours. Take out the bird and let it cool, allowing the liquor to go on cooking. When the fowl is cold remove the muslin and string, and place it in a mould or bowl. Take the liquor off the fire, and let it half cool, then pour it over the bird and let it set for twelve hours. Take it out of the mould and serve with slices of lemon. The jelly must be very clear and firm.

FRICASSÉE DE POULET.
(*Fricassée* of Fowl or Chicken.)

Cut a fine fresh fowl into pieces and let it

soak in some lukewarm water for an hour, then strain off. Put some fresh butter into a saucepan, but do not let it brown, stir in some flour, and when thoroughly hot pour in some stock, some onions, one of which is stuck over with cloves, a calf's sweetbread, some small mushrooms, a bunch of herbs, salt and pepper. Then add the pieces of fowl, let the whole simmer till quite cooked, take out the bunch of herbs, and bind the sauce with yolks of eggs, some fresh cream, and a few drops of lemon juice. Serve on a dish with the legs and wings on the top. Cover the *fricassée* with its own sauce, with the mushrooms around, and garnish with a large crayfish at each corner of the dish.

POULET À L'ESTRAGON.

(Fowl with Tarragon.)

Cut off the neck of a fowl and truss it with the claws inwards, cover it with a thin slice of fat bacon, and put it into a pan with a bunch of parsley, an onion stuck with two cloves, a small bunch of fresh tarragon, and salt and pepper to taste. Over this pour equal quantities of stock and water, so as to just cover the fowl. Place it in the oven, turn it so as not to brown, and let it cook from three-quarters of an hour to an hour. When cooked, strain off the gravy, skim, and add about two ounces of fresh tarragon leaves, and let the fowl boil up in the sauce. Remove the fowl from the pan, untie it, and serve on a dish with a very little of the sauce poured over it. The rest of the sauce is served in a sauce-boat.

POULET-CHASSEUR.
(Chicken Chasseur.)

Take a chicken—not necessarily of the very finest quality—cut it into pieces and brown thoroughly with a mixture of dripping and butter in an enamelled saucepan. Baste from time to time with a little stock—veal stock is preferable—and when the pieces of chicken are well cooked, let them simmer a few minutes in their own liquor, and bind with the juice of a lemon and two tablespoonfuls of tomato sauce. (See Sauces.) Pour the gravy over the fowl and serve with sippets. About an hour's cooking is necessary for this dish.

POULET-CHASSEUR.
(Another Recipe.)

Prepare as in following recipe, and when the pieces of fowl are thoroughly cooked though not *browned*, take them out and dip them one by one into a beaten egg, roll in fine dry bread crumbs, and fry in boiling fat. Serve with sliced lemon. About three-quarters of an hour's cooking is necessary for this dish.

POULET-VILLEROY.
(Chicken à la Villeroy.)

This may be made with cold *fricassée* chicken.

Roll each piece of chicken thoroughly in the *fricassée* sauce, and dredge with fine bread crumbs. Fry to a light brown in boiling fat, and serve very hot with fried parsley and lemon juice.

Note.—Should there not be sufficient chicken to make a dish, some small pieces of cold veal rolled in bread crumbs and fried with the chicken may be added with excellent results.

POULET À LA MACÉDOINE.
(Chicken à la Macédoine.)

Put a fat chicken into a saucepan with some butter; cook it till tender on both sides, but do not let it brown. Make a light *béchamel* sauce. (See Sauces.) Add to it a *macedoine* (see Vegetables), and let it simmer for fifteen minutes in the sauce. Serve on a deep dish with the chicken in the centre. The gravy from the chicken is served apart.

POULET AUX PETITS-POIS.
(Chicken stewed with Green Peas.)

Cut up a fowl and place it in a saucepan with butter, parsley, and some fresh green peas. When slightly browned stir in a little flour, add some stock, and let the sauce boil down. Serve when thoroughly cooked.

POULET À LA MARENGO.
(Chicken à la Marengo.)

Prepare and cut a fowl as for a *fricassée*. Into a

large frying-pan pour a quarter of a pint of oil and lay in the pieces of fowl, each one separately. Add salt and pepper, one ounce of shallots not chopped, half an ounce of garlic not chopped, a bay leaf, a little thyme, and a bunch of parsley. Let it cook for twenty-five minutes, and be sure that the fowl is done through. Strain it off, and keep hot. Stir some flour into the frying-pan, let it brown for four minutes, adding some stock. Stir on the fire for ten minutes, then strain through a sieve. Serve the fowl on a dish in the same way as a *fricassée*, pouring the sauce over. Garnish with mushrooms.

Note.—The fat is never skimmed off the sauce of *Poulet Marengo*.

POULET EN MARINADE.
(Chicken en Marinade.)

Cold roast fowl may be dressed in this manner— Take the pieces of fowl and let them soak for an hour or two in a pan with a little stock, two large spoonfuls of vinegar, salt, pepper, and sweet herbs. Then strain off the pieces of fowl, roll them in a good frying paste, and fry them a good brown in boiling lard. Serve on a folded napkin, and garnish with bunches of parsley.

POULET EN SALADE.
(Chicken Salad.)

Take the remains of a cold roast fowl, cut them into

small pieces about three or four inches square, put them into a salad bowl, add chopped anchovies, sliced gherkins, some stoned olives, some quartered hard boiled eggs, and the hearts of two lettuces cut into small pieces. Dress as an ordinary salad, adding a layer of mayonnaise sauce over the mixture. Then serve.

POULET À LA BOURGUIGNONNE.
(Fowl à la Bourguignonne.)

Bleed a fowl, put the blood in a bowl, and stir for two minutes with a wooden spoon, so that it does not turn into clots. Prepare and cut up the fowl as for a *fricassée*. Melt a large piece of butter in a frying-pan, putting in the pieces of fowl one by one, and adding salt and pepper. When the fowl has browned on both sides, sprinkle with flour and stir for three minutes. Then add a tumblerful of stock, half a tumblerful of red wine, a bunch of herbs, about one pound of small onions previously fried in butter, and about fifteen mushrooms previously prepared (see page 153). Cook on a slow fire for half an hour, and bind with the blood of the fowl. Serve in the same manner as a *fricassée*. This dish must be strongly seasoned.

POULET À LA BONNE FEMME.
(Fowl à la Bonne Femme.)

Prepare a fowl as for a *fricassée*. Put five ounces of butter in a saucepan, three ounces of carrots cut into rings, and the same quantity of onions cut into rings. Let the mixture cook for five minutes, stirring meanwhile, then add the pieces of fowl with salt and pepper to taste. Let it cook another five minutes, and continue stirring. Add some flour, one pint and a half of good stock, and about five ounces of fresh tomatoes cut into pieces, previously skinned and trimmed. Stir until it boils up, then let it simmer for twenty minutes. Add about three-quarters of a pound of small mushrooms and a spoonful of chopped parsley. Let it boil for ten minutes, then serve like a *fricassée*.

POULET EN SAUCE TOMATE.
(Fowl à la Sauce Tomate.)

Prepare a fowl as for *poulet à l'estragon*, but do not put in the tarragon leaves, and serve with tomato sauce poured over the fowl.

POULET AU BLANC.
(Fowl au Blanc.)

Prepare as for *poulet à l'estragon*, and pour over some sauce *poulette* (see page 17). Garnish with mushrooms.

FRITOTS DE POULET.
(Fritots of Chicken.)

The remains of cold roast poultry may be used in several ways. Fritots are an excellent preparation. Here are two recipes for them.

First Recipe.

Cut up the fowl into regular pieces; remove the skin and the gristle, and flatten them out with the flat side of a broad chopper. Let them soak for an hour in some olive oil, salt, pepper, sliced carrots, and chopped parsley, &c. Then dry them; roll them in flour or white bread crumbs, and fry in butter or on the grill. Serve with lemon juice or tomato sauce. (See Sauces.)

Second Recipe.

Soak the pieces of fowl in a little stock for some time, dry them, roll them into beaten egg and into white bread crumbs, repeating the operation twice, fry brown, and serve as above.

CHAUD-FROID DE VOLAILLE.
(Chaud-froid of Chicken.)

Make a good meat jelly. When half cooked mix in a *sauce roux* (see Sauces). Soak each piece of fowl thoroughly in this sauce, and serve *en rocher*, *i.e.*, one piece on the top of another in a heap until a large pile is formed, and pour the rest of the *chaud-froid* over the chicken. Garnish with sliced truffles and gherkins, stoned olives, small mushrooms, &c.

ASPIC DE VOLAILLE.
(Aspic of Fowl.)

Make a good meat jelly; when half cold

spread a layer of it on a small mould and let it set slightly; then lay in the pieces of fowl, and fill up the mould with the rest of the jelly. When thoroughly set, turn out of the mould and serve.

SOUFFLÉS DE VOLAILLE.
(Soufflé of Chicken.)

Chop up some cold chicken with a little bacon and parsley; then pound it in a mortar. Add four spoonfuls of cold *bêchamel sauce* (see Sauces), and the yolks of four eggs. Mix well together and put aside. Three-quarters of an hour before serving beat up the whites and add to the fowl. Pour the mixture into a soufflé mould, buttered and dredged with bread crumbs, or into several small soufflé moulds. Put the moulds into the *bain-marie*, and put the *bain-marie* into the oven. When the soufflé has risen and is cooked, it may be taken out of the mould and served with tomato sauce (see Sauces), or if served in the small moulds a little *Pâté de foie gras* and a few slices of truffles may be added before cooking. Time allowed for cooking, ten minutes.

DUCKS.

CANARD AUX NAVETS.
(Duck with Turnips.)

Truss a very young duck and brown it in a saucepan with two ounces of butter, salt and pepper. Take the duck out of the saucepan and place it on a plate. Stir some flour into the butter for three minutes, then pour in two tumblerfuls of stock, and let it boil for five minutes. Then put the duck back into the saucepan with a bunch of herbs and an onion stuck with two cloves. Cook over a slow fire for three-quarters of an hour. Add about one pound of previously parboiled turnips. When cooked, take out the bunch of herbs and onions, untie the duck, and serve on a dish, pouring the sauce over it and garnishing with the turnips.

CANARD AUX PETITS-POIS.
(Duck with Green Peas.)

Prepare as for preceding recipe. Boil a quarter of a pound of bacon cut into small dice about an inch square. Then fry them in butter, and when browned, dredge with flour and stir for three minutes. Add two tumblerfuls of stock, one onion stuck with two cloves, a bunch of herbs, salt and pepper. Stir until it boils, then add the duck, with one quart of peas. Then let the whole simmer for an hour and a quarter, half covering the saucepan. Take out the onion and the bunch of herbs. Serve the duck on the peas. Garnish with the dice of bacon.

CANARD AUX OLIVES.
(Duck with Olives.)

Prepare the duck as for *Canard aux Navets*, making the same sauce. Take forty stoned olives and let them boil for five minutes in the sauce. Then serve the duck and garnish with the olives.

SALMIS DE CANARD.
(Duck en Salmis.)

This may be made with the remains of some cold roast duck. Take a tumblerful of claret, the same quantity of stock, two spoonfuls of olive oil, and some chopped shallots. Put this in a saucepan and let it boil, then simmer down. Cover the pieces of duck with bread crumbs and warm them in this sauce, pressing the juice of one lemon over the dish before serving. The oil may be replaced by butter.

PIGEONS.

(Stewed Pigeons.)

Fry some small white onions and bacon cut into dice; when browned take them out of the saucepan and replace them by a pigeon. Cook it till brown on both sides, then take it out; stir some flour with stock, salt, pepper, a bunch of herbs, then add the pigeon, bacon, and onions, and a little later on a few parboiled mushrooms. When cooked, take out the bunch of herbs, untie the pigeon, and serve.

PIGEONS À LA CRAPAUDINE.
(Pigeons à la Crapaudine.)

Split the pigeons into two, flatten them out, salt and pepper them, then soak them in warm butter, cover with bread crumbs, cook them on the grill, and serve with *piquanté* sauce.

PIGEONS AUX PETITS-POIS.
(Pigeons stewed with Green Peas.)

Cook the pigeons in butter and bacon cut into dice. When brown stir in a spoonful of flour, add stock and a bunch of parsley, and some medium-sized green peas. Let them cook on a slow fire, and just before serving stir in a little sifted sugar.

PIGEON AUX POINTES D'ASPERGES.
(Pigeons stewed with Asparagus tops.)

Prepare as in preceding recipe, substituting parboiled asparagus tops for green peas. Less time is required for the cooking of the asparagus, so that they need not be added till the pigeon is almost cooked.

PIGEONS FRITS.
(Fried Pigeons.)

Take some young pigeons about eight or ten days old, singe them, and leave their wings, heads, and legs. Cook them in white wine with butter, a bunch of herbs, salt, peppercorns, and some nutmeg. When done, take them out, drain and dry them. Then dip them in some batter, and fry in boiling lard, serving with fried parsley.

GAME.

COLD VENISON.

Cold roast venison may be served with *Poivrade* sauce.

ROUELLES DE CERF À LA SAINT-HUBERT.

(Sliced Haunch of Venison à la Saint Hubert.)

Cut the haunch of venison into large pieces, lard with thick strips of bacon, brown in butter, and add equal quantities of stock and claret, season with salt and pepper, a bunch of herbs, cook for fifteen minutes on a slow fire, and bind with a *roux*, adding a piece of sugar and some gherkins. Serve with stewed prunes.

CIVET DE LIÈVRE.

(Civet of Hare.)

Cut a hare into pieces about four inches square, put the blood in a bowl. Fry some bacon cut into dice. When browned take it out, and into the same saucepan put the pieces of hare, and cook over a very quick fire. Dredge with flour and stir for some moments. Then add a bottle of claret, and about half the same quantity of stock. Season with pepper, spices, a bunch of herbs, and one onion stuck with cloves, and let it cook slowly for two or three hours. Meanwhile fry a quart of small onions in some butter. When well browned sprinkle with a little sifted sugar, pour over some stock, and let them boil down; also parboil a few mushrooms. When the hare is cooked take out the onion and the bunch of herbs, put in the small onions and mushrooms, and serve hot. Just before serving bind the sauce with the blood of the hare, and add some small pieces of butter and stir well.

LIÈVRE EN DAUBE.
(Hare en daube.)

Bone a hare, crush the bones of the head, add a knuckle of veal cut into pieces, carrots, and onions, and let it simmer for an hour and a half over a slow fire, in equal quantities of stock and white wine, with salt and pepper, cloves, and a bunch of herbs. Then take it off the fire and strain the gravy. Cover the bottom of a deep baking-dish with slices of bacon, lay in the pieces of hare, alternated with slices of bacon and a fillet of veal. Add salt, pepper, and spices, and the gravy in which the bones have been cooked. Cover with strips of fat bacon, and cook in a very slow oven. This dish must be served cold.

LAPIN.

GIBELOTTE DE L'APEREAUX.
(Gibelotte of Young Rabbit.)

Cut some rabbits into pieces two and three inches square. Brown some bacon cut into dice in a saucepan. Take them out and put them on a plate, and put the pieces of rabbit into the saucepan, and brown them for seven or eight minutes. Dredge with flour, and add the bacon with equal quantities of stock and white wine, salt and pepper, and a bunch of herbs. Let it cook for twenty-five minutes. Add some parboiled mushrooms, let it simmer for a few moments longer, take out the bunch of herbs, and serve.

LAPIN SAUTÉ.
(Rabbit Sauté.)

Prepare as for *Gibelotte*. Put in a frying-pan a piece of butter, a little olive oil, salt, pepper, and spices, warm them, then add the pieces of rabbit. Let them cook on a quick fire for twenty minutes. Dredge with flour. Add equal quantities of stock and white wine, chopped shallots, and parsley, let it boil up again, and serve.

LAPEREAUX SAUCE TOMATE.
(Young Rabbit à la Sauce Tomate.)

Take the remains of some cold roast rabbit, press them out, and dip them into beaten egg. Fry them a good brown colour in butter, and serve in tomato sauce.

SALMIS DE FAISAN.
(Salmis of Pheasant.)

Cut the remains of a roasted pheasant into pieces. Crush the liver into some stock with a small glassful of white wine, salt, pepper, and nutmeg. Let this mixture boil for a quarter of an hour, then strain it off, and warm up the pieces of pheasant in it. Garnish with small sippets.

PERDRIX À L'ESTOUFADE.
(Partridge à l'Estoufade.)

Crush the partridges with the feet inwards, lard with fat bacon, and season with pepper and salt. Put them into a saucepan with onions, carrots, slices of bacon, a bunch of herbs, and equal parts of stock and white wine. Cook over a slow fire, and serve with its own sauce, boil down, and strain.

PERDRIX AUX CHOUX.
(Partridges with Cabbage.)

Carefully truss a couple of partridges. Strain off a couple of parboiled cabbages, cut off the stems; parboil some lean bacon and some carrots.

Make a *roux* in a large saucepan, place in the cabbages cut into four, the bacon cut into dice, some carrots, a few rinds of raw *saucisson*, a bunch of herbs, an onion stuck with cloves. Season with salt and pepper.

Bury the partridges in the midst of the cabbages, cover with a little dripping, add in a glassful or two of good stock, cover with a thick sheet of white paper, then put on the lid, and let the dish cook very slowly for two or three hours. The liquid must be entirely absorbed by the cabbages. Serve the partridges breast upwards on a thick layer of the cabbages. Garnish with the other ingredients. A good *roux* sauce, to which some stock has been added, is served with the dish.

MAUVIETTES RÔTIES.
(Broiled Larks.)

Remove the gizzards of six larks by making a small incision under the leg and pressing out the gizzard, taking care not to tear the flesh of the bird. Around each bird wrap a thin slice of fat bacon. Place them on a skewer in a row, slightly separating each bird from the other. Cook over a quick fire or in the oven for eight minutes. Serve with their own gravy, and garnish with watercress.

SALMIS DE MAUVIETTES.
(Salmis of Larks.)

Take out the gizzards of twelve larks, which make

a dish sufficient for four people. Put the larks into a saucepan with some dice of bacon previously browned in an ounce of butter, with half a pound of sliced mushrooms. Cook for eight minutes, and stir in a little flour. Pour in a glassful of white wine, which has been previously boiled for five minutes, with a very little salt and some pepper, stirring meanwhile. Add a teaspoonful of chopped parsley, let it boil up, and then serve.

BÉCASSES RÔTIES.
(Roasted Snipe.)

Snipe must not be trussed. Cook in the same way as larks, and serve on fried toast.

Snipe may also be served *en salmis*.

SALMIS DE BÉCASSES AU CHASSEUR.
(Salmis of Snipe au Chasseur.)

Cut the snipe into pieces and put it into a saucepan with two large table-spoonfuls of olive oil. Add a glassful of red wine, chopped shallot, and parsley, salt, and pepper. Let it boil for some time. Strain the sauce through a sieve, dredge with fine dry bread crumbs, adding a piece of butter and the juice of a lemon. Warm up the pieces of snipe in this mixture and serve.

SALMIS DE BÉCASSES À L'ESPRIT-DE-VIN.
(Salmis of Snipe in chafing-dish.)

This is prepared in a chafing-dish on the table.

Put in a small piece of butter, the pieces of snipe, with salt, pepper, chopped shallots, a glassful of white wine, the juice of a lemon. Dredge with fine bread crumbs, and let the pieces of snipe bake for ten minutes, browning on both sides.

CAILLES RÔTIES.
(Roast Quails.)

Wrap each quail into a vine leaf, and then into a thin slice of fat bacon. Skewer them, and let them cook for twenty minutes.

CAILLES AUX PETITS-POIS.
(Quails with Green Peas.)

In a saucepan lay a slice of veal and a slice of ham, some carrots and onions cut into rings, and a bunch of herbs. Upon this place a couple of quails, cover with strips of bacon and a sheet of thick white paper. Cook in the oven, and serve covered with green peas previously cooked.

CAILLES AUX LAITUES.
(Quails with Stewed Lettuce.)

Cook as in previous recipe. Just before serving take the hearts of four lettuces previously parboiled, and cook them in the sauce of the quails. Serve.

SARCELLES.
(Teal.)

Teal may be cooked *à la broche* like quails or larks.

It may be served with olives or turnips, or made *en pâté*.

SARCELLES AUX OLIVES.
(Teal with Olives.)

Cook the teal in its own fat, then grill. Stone some olives, wash them in cold water, let them simmer for some time in stock, and serve with the teal.

PLUVIERS RÔTIS.
(Roast Plovers.)

Wrap each plover in a sheet of buttered paper, grill them on a skewer, and serve on fried toast.

PLUVIERS BRAISÉS.
(Braised Plovers.)

Braise the plovers between slices of bacon, with sweet herbs, onions, carrots, thyme, and bay leaf, nutmeg, salt, and pepper. Moisten with stock, cook for two hours, and serve with its own gravy strained through a sieve.

PLUVIERS AU GRATIN.
(Plovers au gratin.)

Make a *farce* (stuffing) with the inside of the plovers, and some bacon, parsley, shallots, bread crumbs very finely minced and mixed together with salt and pepper. Stuff the plovers with a portion of this mixture, and serve them on the remainder. Bake the plovers in the oven, covered with strips of bacon. Serve with Italian sauce.

Plovers may also be braised.

GRIVE.
(Thrush.)

There are two sorts of thrushes, the larger feeds upon juniper berries, the smaller upon grapes.

GRIVE RÔTÈ.
(Roast Thrush.)

Do not truss them. Stuff with a few juniper berries if of the larger kind; wrap in a vine leaf if of the smaller kind. In both cases, wrap in a slice of fat bacon, and roast for fifteen minutes, serve on fried toast.

SALMIS DE GRIVES.
(Salmis of Thrushes.)

See *Alouettes en Salmis*. They are prepared in the same way.

ORTOLANS.
(Ortolans.)

These birds are cooked in the same manner as larks and thrushes.

ASPARAGUS.

POINTES D'ASPERGES AU JUS.
(Asparagus Tops au Jus.)

Cut some fat bacon into small dice and mix it with chopped parsley and chervil, salt and pepper, and the tops of some fresh asparagus; cook in stock over a slow fire, skim, and serve with thick gravy.

ARTICHOKES.

ARTICHAUTS SAUCE BLANCHE.
(Artichokes with White Sauce.)

Trim some artichokes, cut off the stalks, wash with care, and put them into a saucepan full of boiling salted water. When cooked, throw them into cold water. Take out the hay, put them back into boiling water, strain them off, serve with *sauce blanche* in a sauce-boat (see Sauces, page 12), or a mixture of oil and vinegar, pepper, and salt, mixed on each plate.

Note.—To trim an artichoke, cut about an inch off each leaf with a pair of scissors, so as to give a rounded effect to the vegetable.

ARTICHAUTS GRILLÉS À LA PROVENÇALE.
(Grilled Artichokes à la Provençale.)

Parboil the artichokes, trim them and take out the hay, strain them off, and soak them in some good olive oil with a little salt. Fill up the cavity left by the removal of the hay with a spoonful of oil, salt, pepper, chopped spring onions and parsley, and a few light bread crumbs. Cook them on the grill.

When well browned, another spoonful of olive oil may be poured over them if desired.

ARTICHAUTS FRITS.
(Fried Artichokes.)

Trim some artichokes, and cut them into slices from the top to the bottom; wash them in vinegar and water, strain them off, dip them in some batter, and fry them in oil or lard. Strain them off before the fire, and serve them in a heap very hot with fried parsley and a sprinkling of salt.

BEIGNETS D'ARTICHAUTS A LA CLAIRE.
(Artichoke Fritters à la Claire.)

Take the hearts of some fresh boiled artichokes, cut them into round slices about three-quarters of an inch thick, dip them into frying batter, and fry them in boiling oil or lard. Serve hot with a sprinkling of sauce. Garnish with lemons cut into quarters.

ARTICHAUTS À LA BARIGOULE.
(Artichokes à la Barigoule.)

Trim and parboil some artichokes; remove the hay and replace it by a *farce* composed of chopped mushrooms, shallots, and parsley, fat bacon cut into very small dice, salt, and pepper. This *farce* must be fried in butter first, then put into the cup of each artichoke in a small heap. Then cover each artichoke with a thin strip of fat bacon about three inches long; tie it up carefully with fine string, so that it may not fall to pieces in the cooking, then lay each artichoke very carefully on to the bottom of a deep pan or cooking-dish, and pour over some good stock or gravy, Bovril, &c., so that the artichokes are not submerged, but are barely covered. Bake in the oven for twenty minutes, and serve.

ARTICHAUTS EN FRICASSÉE DE POULET.
(Artichokes en *Fricassée* de Poulet.)

Prepare the artichokes for frying, cook them in salted boiling water, strain off and throw them into cold water, strain off again and dress them *en fricassée de poulet*. (See recipe.)

ARTICHAUTS À LA BONNE FEMME.
(Artichokes à la Bonne Femme.)

Prepare the artichokes as for *la sauce blanche* (see p. 12). Serve them boiling on to a very hot dish, and over them pour some *white sauce*, or a sauce *ravigote* (see Sauces), or some thick rich gravy.

Note.—The sauce must be poured over the vegetable so as to entirely soak it.

ARTICHAUTS SAUCE POIVRADE OU À L'HUILE.
(Artichokes à la Sauce Poivrade.)

Take some very young and tender artichokes, cut

them into pieces or slices from top to bottom, and serve them raw in a side dish with a *sauce poivrade* or *sauce à l'huile* in a sauce-boat.

AUBERGINES OR EGG-PLANTS.

This vegetable is shaped somewhat like a thick cucumber, and is of a deep red purplish colour.

AUBERGINES À LA PROVENÇALE.
(Egg-Plant à la Provençale.)

Divide the egg-plant into two halves, take out the seed and make several incisions lengthwise with a sharp knife; sprinkle with salt and put them aside for half an hour. Squeeze them so as to press out the water, salt and pepper them, pour over a little olive oil, sprinkle with some chopped parsley, and cook on the grill.

AUBERGINES FRITES.
(Fried Egg-Plant.)

Peel the vegetables and cut them lengthwise into three or four pieces, make many incisions with a sharp knife, season with salt and pepper, and set them aside for half an hour. Squeeze out the water; then fry them in olive oil, and serve with fried parsley.

AUBERGINE FARCIES.
(Stuffed Egg-Plant.)

Cut the vegetables into halves and parboil them.

Cut out the centres and chop them up finely, mixed with chopped mushrooms, parsley, spring onions, bread crumbs, a few small dice of fat bacon, pepper, salt, and chopped shallots. Fill the cavity in the centre of each half with this *farce*, lay the halves in a baking dish, pour some olive oil over the whole, sprinkle with fine bread crumbs, and brown in the oven. Serve.

SALADE D'AUBERGINES À LA PROVENÇALE.

(Egg-Plant salad à la Provençale.)

Peel some egg-plants, cut them into slices, and let them soak for two hours in vinegar with a strong seasoning of salt and pepper. Take out the pieces, wipe them, and press them hard in a cloth, put them into a salad bowl with some raw rampions with some fresh watercress, hard-boiled eggs, stoned olives, and a few pieces of tunny fish. Mix with oil, vinegar, pepper, salt, and a spoonful of French mustard.

BEETROOTS.

BETTERAVES EN SALADE.
(Beetroot Salad.)

(See Salads.)

BETTERAVE À LA CRÊME.
(Beetroot à la Crême.)

Peel and slice a beetroot previously parboiled. Cook the slices over a slow fire in a *béchamel* sauce (see p. 14). A few unripe muscatel grapes cooked in the béchamel also give an excellent flavouring to this dish.

BETTERAVES À LA POITEVINE.
(Beetroot à la Poitevine.)

Cook some beetroots in the oven, peel them and cut into slices. Make a *roux*, add half a pint of water or stock, place in the slices of beetroot with some parboiled chopped onions; season with spices, and just before serving, stir in half a teaspoonful of strong vinegar.

BETTERAVES À LA CHARTREUSE.
(Beetroot à la Chartreuse.)

Cut some yellow beetroots into slices, sandwich

a piece of raw onion in between two slices of the beetroot, taking out the centre of the onion. Dip the sandwich into batter, and sprinkle it with finely chopped chervil, pimpernel, grated nutmeg, and a little salt, and fry a golden brown in boiling fat. Serve with a sprinkling of salt, and garnish with fried parsley.

CARDOONS.

CARDONS AU MAIGRE.
(Cardoons au maigre.)

Wash and prepare some cardoons, cut into pieces and put them into boiling water with some salt and a spoonful of flour. Stir until cooked. Then strain them off, and serve with a white sauce poured over them.

CARDONS AU GRAS.
(Cardoons au Gras.)

Prepare as in above recipe, and serve with roux sauce mixed with some good stock, and poured over the vegetable.

CARDONS AU GRATIN.
(Cardoons au gratin.)

Prepare the cardoons as for *Cardons au maigre* (see above). Butter a nickel baking-dish (plat au gratin) and sprinkle it with dried bread crumbs, lay in the cardoons, then sprinkle again with bread crumbs, pour over some melted butter, and brown in the oven.

CARDONS AU L'ITALIENNE.
(Cardoons à l'Italienne.)

Same as preceding recipe with the addition of grated parmesan cheese added to the bread crumbs.

CARDONS À LA POULETTE.
(Cardoons à la Poulette.)

Prepare as for Cardons au maigre (see recipe, page 124). Put a piece of butter mixed with flour into a saucepan, stir in some cream and put in the cardoons. Bind the sauce with yolks of eggs and a few drops of lemon juice or vinegar.

CAPSICUMS OR CHILIS.

These are generally used for flavouring or are pickled to be eaten with cold meats. The sweeter kinds of capsicums are, however, excellent when served as *hors-d'œuvres*.

PIMENTS EN HORS-D'ŒUVRE.
(Capsicum or sweet Chilien hors d'œuvre.)

Split the vegetable in two and grill it over the fire. Remove the outer skin and chop it up not too finely. Put it into a *ravier* or side dish, and dredge it with salt. Pour oil and vinegar over it, and serve.

LETTUCES.

LAITUES AU JUS.
(Lettuces stewed in Gravy.)

Take eight young full-bodied lettuces; remove the outer leaves and the yellow skin on the stalk. Parboil for ten minutes, throw them into cold water and press them dry. Cut them into halves lengthwise and then tie them up whole again with fine string. Put them into a saucepan; season with a little salt; cover them with some good stock, and add a little beef dripping, a bunch of herbs, and one onion stuck with two cloves. Cover with a paper under the lid, and let simmer for two hours. When cooked, strain off and untie the pieces of lettuce, and serve them on a dish with thick gravy poured over them. Garnish with sippets.

ONIONS.

PURÉE D'OIGNONS À LA SOUBISE.
(Mashed Onions à la Soubise.)

Peel and finely chop up some white onions; cook them in butter over a very slow fire without allowing them to brown. Add two or three spoonfuls of *haricots blancs en purée* (see recipe, p. 142) and a little grated nutmeg. Pass the mixture through a fine sieve, stir in a small piece of butter, and serve.

RAGOÛT D'OIGNONS.
(Onions en Ragoût.)

Bake some onions in the oven; remove their skins and put them into a saucepan with some gravy or stock, allowing them to simmer for twenty minutes. Bind the sauce with a pinch of flour and a spoonful of French mustard. Serve.

OIGNONS FARCIS.
(Stuffed Onions.)

Peel twenty or thirty large onions; parboil them, throw them into cold water, and strain them off. Bore a hole through the centre of each onion and fill in with a stuffing of forcemeat. Arrange the onions side by side in a saucepan, cover them with slices of bacon, dredge with a little sifted sugar, season with salt, and cook over a quick fire. When the onions are cooked, simmer the sauce for ten minutes, and serve.

OIGNONS GLACÉS.
(Glazed Onions.)

Carefully peel some onions all of one size. Butter the bottom of a saucepan, place in the onions side by side; add a little water, salt, pepper, powdered sugar, and a little more butter. Cover the onions with a piece of white buttered paper before putting on the lid, and put the saucepan on to a quick fire, which may be moderated when the sauce has reduced to half its original quantity. Then let the onions cook slowly until the liquor is reduced to a glaze.

POTATOES.

POMMES DE TERRE EN ROBE DE CHAMBRE.

(Potatoes Boiled in Jackets.)

Boil some potatoes with salt. Do not remove their skins. Serve in a folded napkin with fresh butter handed round.

POMMES DE TERRE EN ROBE DE CHAMBRE.

(Potatoes Baked in Jackets.)

Rub some fine floury potatoes in a cloth, but do not wash them. Bake in a moderate oven until the outer skin has formed a thick crust. Serve with fresh butter handed round.

Note.—In Brittany the tops of the potatoes are cut away; the floury part being removed with a small spoon is then mixed with salt, pepper, and fresh butter, and the potato restuffed; the tops are then replaced, and the potatoes served hot are eaten with spoons like boiled eggs.

POMMES DE TERRÉ À LA MAÎTRE D'HÔTEL.
(Potatoes à la Maître d'Hôtel.)

Wash and boil some potatoes; peel them and cut them into slices. Put them into a saucepan with some butter, chopped parsley and shallot, salt, and pepper, turn them from time to time; bind with another piece of butter and a few drops of lemon juice or of vinegar.

POMMES DE TERRE À LA PARISIENNE.
(Potatoes à la Parisienne.)

Put some butter or dripping into a saucepan, with some onions cut into small dice; let the onion brown; add water or stock; put in the potatoes with salt, pepper, and a bunch of herbs; let cook until quite soft, then serve.

POMMES DE TERRE EN SAUCE BLANCHE.
(Potatoes à la Sauce Blanche.)

Boil some potatoes and remove their skins. Cut into slices and serve with white sauce. (See Sauces, p. 12.)

POMMES DE TERRE AU LARD.
(Potatoes au Lard.)

Brown some dice of bacon in some butter; stir in some flour so as to make a light *roux*, add stock or water; season with salt, pepper, and a bunch of herbs; let the mixture boil for a few moments, and add the potatoes peeled and whole, unless they be very large. When cooked, skim the fat off the sauce, and serve.

POMMES DE TERRE À LA CRÊME.
(Potatoes with Cream.)

Melt a large piece of butter in a saucepan; stir in a spoonful of flour, chopped parsley and shallots, salt, pepper, and grated nutmeg. Mix thoroughly, then pour in some good cream. Stir until boiling point, then add the potatoes previously cooked and cut into slices.

PURÉE DE POMMES DE TERRE.
(Mashed Potatoes.)

Boil some large floury potatoes; strain them off and pass them through a fine tammy. Put the *purée* into a saucepan with a large piece of fresh butter and a cupful of milk or cream. Stir until boiling point. Serve.

PURÉE DE POMMES DE TERRE AU FROMAGE.
(Purée of Potatoes with Cheese.)

Put some *purée* of potatoes into a deep baking-dish. Stir in some grated parmesan cheese. Sprinkle some more parmesan cheese over the top of the dish, add some small pieces of butter, and brown in a quick oven.

SWEET POTATOES.

BEIGNETS DE PATATES.
(Sweet Potato Fritters.)

Wash and scrape the sweet potatoes and cut them into slices lengthwise. Let them soak for half an hour in some brandy with the rind of a lemon. Strain them off, dip them into batter, and fry a light brown. Dredge with sifted sugar, and serve.

PATATES AU BEURRE.
(Sweet Potatoes au Beurre.)

Steam the vegetable until quite tender, then remove their skins; cut them into pieces, and cook them in a saucepan with a little salt and a large piece of butter.

POMMES DE TERRE EN SALADE.
(Potato Salad.)

Cut some cold boiled potatoes into thin slices. Put them into a salad bowl with chopped parsley, salt, pepper, oil, and vinegar. Mix thoroughly. Chopped spring onions may be added if desired.

PEAS.

PETITS-POIS À LA PARISIENNE.
(Small Peas à la Parisienne.)

Put some fresh green peas into a saucepan with a large piece of fresh butter, a little water, a little salt, a good dredging of sifted sugar, a bunch of parsley, and a few small onions. The heart of a fresh lettuce may be added if desired. Cook on a moderate fire for half an hour. Take out the bunch of parsley and the onions. Rub some flour into a piece of butter, stir it into the peas, and serve.

PETITS-POIS AU LARD OU AU JAMBON.
(Green Peas with Bacon or Ham.)

Make a light *roux* and cut up some lean bacon into dices or some sliced ham into small square pieces, and cook it brown in the *roux*. Add some stock and the peas, a bunch of parsley and spring onions, salt, and pepper. Let the peas cook over a moderate fire.

PETITS-POIS À LA CRÊME.
(Green Peas with Cream.)

See recipe *Haricots verts à la crême* (p. 140).

PURÉE DE PETITS-POIS.
(Purée of Green Peas.)

Boil until quite tender some peas of the larger kind. Strain off and pass through a fine sieve. Place in a saucepan with a large lump of butter, salt, and pepper. Stir until boiling point, and serve.

Note.—Except for *Purée de petits pois*, French cooks generally select peas of the very smallest size for the above recipes.

POIS-CHICHES.
(Dried Peas.)

These peas, if previously soaked for several hours, can be made into excellent soups and *purées*. They are also very good when boiled and used half-cold for making salads.

SALSIFIES.

SALSIFIS EN SAUCE BLANCHE.
(Salsifies with White Sauce.)

Scrape the salsifies and let them soak for some time in water with a little vinegar. Cook them in boiling water with vinegar, strain them off, and serve with white butter sauce. (See Sauces, p. 12.)

SALSIFIS FRITS.
(Fried Salsifies.)

Cook the salsifies as in preceding recipe. Let them cool, and dip them one by one in some good frying batter. Fry a light brown, and serve sprinkled with salt.

SALSIFIS À LA CRÊME.
(Salsifies with Cream.)

Cook the salsifies as in preceding recipes and strain them off. Put them into a saucepan with a large piece of butter; stir in a spoonful of flour and a large cupful of cream or milk. Season with salt and grated nutmeg. Let it come to a boil, and serve.

SALSIFIS AU JUS.
(Salsifies with Gravy.)

After boiling the salsifies cook them in a *roux*; mix with some good gravy or stock. Let the sauce simmer for ten minutes, and serve very hot.

SALSIFIS AU BEURRE D'ANCHOIS.
(Salsifies au Beurre d'Anchois.)

Cook some boiled salsifies in a little *roux*, and add to some *beurre d'anchois* (see Sauces) just before serving.

Note.—The young sprouts of salsifies make excellent salads.

SORREL.

PURÉE D'OSEILLE AU GRAS.
(Sorrel en Purée au gras.)

Chop up a little sorrel, some lettuce, a little chervil, and a little white beet, and put them into a saucepan without adding anything else. Stir until the ingredients have almost melted; then put in a large piece of butter, and stir again. Season with salt and pepper. Bind with fresh cream and yolks of three eggs. Serve.

PURÉE D'OSEILLE AU MAIGRE.
(Sorrel en Purée au maigre.)

Melt down a little sorrel as in the preceding recipe, and strain off the water it throws off. Add a large piece of butter, and stir the sorrel almost to boiling point. Serve.

Various meats and fish are served with this dish, which is also often garnished with hard-boiled eggs or fried sippets.

TOMATOES.

TOMATES FARCIS.
(Stuffed Tomatoes.)

Remove the centres and pips of some large tomatoes, not over-ripe. Make a *farce* of sausage meat, chopped parsley and shallots, a small piece of chopped garlic, and some chopped tarragon leaves; season with pepper and salt. Stuff the tomatoes with this *farce* and place them side by side in a deep baking dish, into which a little olive oil has been previously poured. Dredge each tomato with fine dry bread crumbs and cover with a small piece of butter. Cook until brown in a moderate oven, and serve with or without lemon juice.

TOMATES EN SALADE.
(Tomato Salad.)

Put them in boiling water to remove their skins. Cut them into slices and remove the seeds. Cut into very thin slices some white onions or Spanish onions, and in a salad bowl put a layer of onions, another of tomatoes, and so on. Add salt and pepper and a good quantity of vinegar, and put the bowl by for two hours. Then take out the tomatoes, season with oil and vinegar, and serve.

TOMATES EN SALADE.
(Another Recipe.)

Slice some large fresh tomatoes; remove the pips and the cores, and put them into a salad-bowl with some sliced cucumber in about the same proportion. Season with salt, pepper, oil, vinegar, and finely chopped chervil or parsley.

FRENCH BEANS AND SCARLET-RUNNERS.

HARICOTS VERTS À LA POULETTE.
(French Beans à la Poulette.)

Choose some very fine and tender French beans. Pare and wash them, and cook them over a quick fire in some salted boiling water. When cooked, throw them into cold water, and strain them off. Cut an onion into dice, cook it in a large piece of butter, so that it does not brown; when nearly done, stir in a little flour and some stock; put in the beans with salt, pepper, chopped spring onions, and parsley. Just before serving, bind the sauce with yolks of eggs and a few drops of vinegar. The sauce must not be abundant.

HARICOTS VERTS À LA LYONNAISE.
(French Beans à la Lyonnaise.)

Fry some chopped onions in some butter. When browned, add some French beans plainly boiled, and seasoned with salt, pepper, chopped parsley, and spring onions. Let the mixture cook together till slightly browned, turning it in the pan several times. A few minutes before serving, pour in a few drops of vinegar.

HARICOTS VERTS SAUTÉS AU BEURRE.
(Green Beans fried in Butter.)

Put some French beans or scarlet-runners previously parboiled into a large frying-pan with two ounces of butter. Cook them over a quick fire for eight or ten minutes, turning them in the pan during the whole process of cooking. Add a pinch of salt, half a spoonful of chopped parsley, and a teaspoonful of lemon juice. Mix thoroughly and serve.

HARICOTS BLANCS FRAIS À LA MAÎTRE D'HÔTEL.
(New White Beans à la Maître d'Hôtel.)

Take some new white beans freshly shelled, and cook them in cold water with salt and a piece of butter. Carefully skim the liquor and let the beans simmer for some time, then strain off and put them into a saucepan with some butter *à la maître d'hôtel*. (See Sauces, p. 13.)

HARICOTS FLAGEOLETS À LA MAÎTRE D'HÔTEL.
(Green Haricot Beans à la Maître d'Hôtel.)

Green haricot beans or *flageolets* are in season from the 1st of July to the 15th of October. They must be of a tender pale green colour. Prepare as in preceding recipe, and serve with lemon cut into quarters. When *flageolets* are bought tinned, they must be previously washed in boiling water before they are cooked.

HARICOTS PANACHÉS.
(Mixed Beans.)

Parboil equal quantities of green *flageolets* and French beans. Strain them off, and put into a saucepan with a large piece of fresh butter, salt, pepper, and chopped parsley. Just before serving, stir in a little milk or cream, and serve hot with or without lemon juice.

HARICOTS SOISSONS AU LARD.
(Kidney Beans with Bacon.)

Wash some kidney beans, and let them soak for two hours or more in cold water. Strain them off and cook them in water with some slices of bacon cut into dice, pepper and salt, an onion stuck with cloves, and a bunch of sweet herbs. The beans are cooked when they can be crushed between the thumb and first finger, and great care must be taken not to let them be over-cooked. The quantity of water used for cooking the beans must be only just sufficient to be soaked up.

PURÉE DE HARICOTS BLANCS.
(Purée of White Beans.)

Let the beans soak in cold water for two hours, then boil up with water and salt. Let them cook for several hours until quite soft, then press them through a tammy. Put the *purée* into a saucepan with a large piece of fresh butter, stir in a cupful of milk, and serve. This *purée* is excellent when served with roast mutton.

SALADE DE HARICOTS BLANCS.
(Salad of White Beans.)

Take some cold boiled beans and mix in a salad-bowl with oil, vinegar, pepper, salt, and chopped parsley.

Lentils also make excellent salads.

SALADE DE HARICOTS VERTS.
(Salad of French Beans.)

Prepare as in preceding recipe.

LENTILS.

Lentils are prepared in the same manner as kidney beans. They make excellent soups and salads. Lentils *en purée* are served with braised meats and roast mutton.

PURÉE DE LENTILLES.
(Purée of Lentils.)

This is prepared in exactly the same manner as the *purée* of white beans. (See recipe, p. 142.)

CRESSES.

These are of two kinds—watercress and garden cress. Both are used for salads. (See Salads, p. 165.)

SPINACH.

ÉPINARDS À LA MAÎTRE D'HÔTEL.
(Spinach à la Maître d'Hôtel.)

Remove the stems of the spinach, wash the leaves, cook them in boiling water with a little salt; then plunge them into cold water, strain them off and chop them up. Put them into a saucepan with salt, peppercorns, and grated nutmeg. When they are thoroughly warmed up, stir in a large piece of butter until it melts. Then serve.

ÉPINARDS À L'ANCIENNE.
(Spinach à l'Ancienne.)

Prepare and parboil the spinach as in preceding recipe, chop it up fine, and put it into a saucepan with butter, salt, and grated nutmeg. Stir in a large piece of butter mixed with flour, a little sifted sugar and a cupful of cream. Stir during the whole process of cooking, and serve with fried sippets of bread.

RISSOLES D'ÉPINARDS.
(Rissoles of Spinach.)

Cold boiled spinach, finely mashed and mixed with cold mashed potatoes or fresh bread crumbs mixed in milk, make excellent rissoles. Bind with yolk of eggs, roll into balls, dredge with bread crumbs, and fry in butter or boiling lard.

ÉPINARDS AU JUS.

Parboil and chop up the spinach; put it into a saucepan with grated nutmeg, some pepper, and a large piece of butter; stir in some veal stock or rich gravy and another piece of fresh butter just before serving. Garnish with fried sippets.

FÈVES.
(Broad Beans.)

When the broad beans are very young and tender they may be eaten in the complete state. When they become larger and coarser, the outer skin must be removed when the vegetable is parboiled.

FÈVES À LA CRÊME.
(Broad Beans à la Crême.)

Boil the beans, throw them into cold water, and strain them off. Cook them in butter that has not burnt brown. Season with salt, pepper, chopped parsley, and a bunch of savoy (this is indispensable). Stir in a little flour and some stock. Just before serving, stir in some fresh cream, warm it up without allowing it to boil, then serve.

PURÉE DE FÈVES.
(Broad Beans en Purée.)

Boil the beans with a little salt, throw them into

cold water, and then strain off. Remove their skins and pound the beans in a mortar, or failing that, thoroughly mash with a fork. Melt a large piece of butter in a saucepan, put in the beans with pepper and salt, pour in a cupful of milk, and stir gently and unceasingly until boiling point, then serve.

POMMES-PAILLES.
(Potato Straws.)

Cut some potatoes into long thin strips, a little broader than coarse straw. Cook them in *boiling* fat till brown, strain off carefully, then serve.

POMMES SOUFFLÉES.
(Blown Potatoes.)

Cut some potatoes into *very* thin slices, throw them into boiling fat, and when half-cooked, take out and throw into cold water. Strain off, and throw back into a fresh lot of boiling fat. Each piece of potato must be blown out like an air ball. Serve hot.

PURÉE DE MARRONS.
(Chestnuts en Purée.)

Remove the outer skin of some fine chestnuts, boil in water until quite soft; strain off and remove the second skin. Pass through a sieve and prepare as for *purée d'haricots blancs* (see p. 142). This dish is excellent served with roast mutton.

TURNIPS.

NAVETS À LA BÉCHAMEL.
(Turnips à la Béchamel.)

Peel and parboil some fresh turnips; cook them in stock and serve with sauce *à la béchamel* (see Sauces, p. 14) served over them.

NAVETS AU JUS.
(Turnips au Jus.)

Peel and trim some turnips; parboil them and strain off. Put them into a saucepan with a little butter and powdered sugar. When the turnips are sufficiently browned, add some gravy or strong stock, salt, pepper, and a bunch of herbs. When cooked, reduce the sauce to half its original quantity, and just before serving, stir in a little rich gravy or a piece of butter.

PURÉE DE NAVETS.
(Turnips en Purée.)

Boil some turnips until quite tender, strain off, and pass through a tammy or mash thoroughly with a fork. Warm up in a saucepan with a large piece of butter and a little milk, stirring through the whole process of cooking.

NAVETS GLACÉS.

(Glazed Turnips.)

Trim twelve or fifteen fine turnips of an equal size; parboil, then strain off. Butter the bottom of a large saucepan and place in the turnips side by side. Add some good stock, a little salt, a little sifted sugar, and a little mace. When the turnips have come to a boil, cover them with a piece of thick white buttered paper, placed under the lid of the saucepan; draw the saucepan on to the front of the fire, and put a few red-hot coals on the lid or a hot shovel. When the turnips are cooked, uncover the saucepan and let the sauce reduce to a glaze. Arrange the turnips on an open dish; stir a little stock into the saucepan so as to remove the glaze; take out the mace and pour the liquid in the saucepan over the turnips. Serve.

NAVETS À LA POULETTE.

(Turnips à la Poulette.)

Trim about thirty small turnips; boil them and strain off. Put a large piece of fresh butter into a saucepan, stir in a spoonful of flour, but do not let the sauce brown; add some stock and throw in the turnips. Let the sauce simmer, then add a little powdered sugar. Just before serving, bind with yolks of eggs and a piece of fresh butter.

NAVETS AU SUCRE.
(Turnips with Sugar.)

Pare and trim some small turnips; brown them in butter, dredge them with powdered sugar, add a little salt and two large spoonfuls of stock. Cover the pan and let them cook on a slow fire.

CUCUMBERS.

CONCOMBRES AU BLANC.
(Cucumbers au Blanc.)

Cut the cucumbers into four or eight pieces, peel them, take out the seeds, and parboil them for five minutes in salted boiling water. Take them out and put them into cold water, strain off and put them into a saucepan with some melted butter; stir in a little flour, add stock, and cook on a slow fire. When cooked, add some milk or some cream and some chopped parsley. Bind with yolks of eggs and some drops of vinegar. Serve.

CONCOMBRES À L'ITALIENNE.
(Cucumbers à l'Italienne.)

Proceed as in above recipe, adding grated parmesan cheese to the cream or milk.

CONCOMBRES FARCIS.
(Stuffed Cucumbers.)

Cut the ends of the cucumbers and empty them by means of a small spoon. Peel them and parboil them in boiling water with a few drops of vinegar and some salt. When cooked, dip them into cold water and strain them off. Stuff them with a farce composed of the crumbs of a French roll soaked in milk, chopped shallot and parsley, pepper and salt, and a little sausage meat if desired. (The farce must be previously cooked with a little butter.) Lay the stuffed cucumbers in a baking-dish, cover with stock, bread crumbs, and a little butter. Brown in the oven, and serve.

CONCOMBRES EN SALADE.
(Cucumber Salad.)

(See Salads, p. 165.)

MUSHROOMS.

Mushrooms may be cooked in various ways, and are greatly used in garnishing different dishes. When used for garnishing, they must be cooked in salt water with a little vinegar and a piece of butter. After boiling a few moments, they must be taken off the fire and left in their own liquor till used.

CHAMPIGNONS À LA PROVENÇALE.
(Mushrooms à la Provençale.)

Take some large ordinary English mushrooms, or the French kind called *cèpes*, which may be bought in England tinned, preserved in oil. Clean and trim the mushrooms, cut off the stalks, and cook them over a slow fire, with olive oil, and half a tumblerful of white wine. Arrange them on a shallow baking-dish, chop up the stalks and put them into a small saucepan with some butter, chopped parsley, one or two boned and pounded anchovies, and a little garlic if liked. The crumb of a French roll soaked in milk may also be added if liked. Mix up all these ingredients together so as to form a *farce*, and place a small heap of the *farce* on each upturned mushroom. Dredge with fine bread crumbs, and brown in the oven. Melted butter may be substituted for the oil.

CHAMPIGNONS À LA POULETTE.
(Mushrooms à la Poulette.)

Cook as for garnishing; strain them off and put them into a saucepan with a piece of butter and a spoonful of flour, add a little water or stock, and stir during the whole process of cooking. Bind with the yolk of eggs and a few drops of vinegar. Serve hot.

CROÛTES AUX CHAMPIGNONS.
(Mushrooms on Toast.)

Prepare them as for *à la poulette*, with very good stock. Place each mushroom separately upon a slice of toasted or fried bread.

MORILLES SAUTÉES.
(Moril Mushrooms.)

Cut some moril mushrooms into halves and soak them in lukewarm water for ten minutes, strain off and cook them for another ten minutes with butter, lemon juice, a little grated nutmeg, a little powdered sugar, salt, and pepper; then cover with gravy or rich stock, add a bunch of parsley and an onion stuck with cloves. Let it cook for another half-hour. Take out the onion and herbs and add a few drops of vinegar.

CABBAGES.

The best kind of cabbages are those that are known as savoy cabbages.

CHOU AU LARD.
(Cabbage with Bacon.)

Parboil the cabbage, cut it into four pieces, and put it into an earthen pan, with a small piece of lean bacon, a *saucisson*, and a few slices of fat bacon. Cover with water and add pepper and nutmeg. Let it come to a boil, then simmer. When cooked, take out the cabbage and bacon and let the sauce simmer, binding it when still on the fire with a piece of butter and a little flour. Pour the sauce over the cabbage, and serve.

CHOU FARCI.
(Stuffed Cabbage.)

Remove the outer leaves, parboil the cabbage, remove the heart, and press the cabbage so as to extract all water. Prepare some sausage meat mixed with the yolks of four eggs and a little beef marrow, and fill up the void in the centre of the cabbage with this *farce*. Spread a spoonful of *farce* under each leaf. Press the cabbage into its original shape, and tie with fine string not too tightly. Put the stuffed cabbage back into the saucepan with a small saveloy sausage, a bunch of herbs, onions, carrots, grated nutmeg, and a few peppercorns; cover with a few slices of fat bacon and some stock. When cooked, untie the cabbage and serve in its own liquor mixed with a little gravy.

CHOU AU GRATIN.
(Cabbages au gratin.)

Put the remains of a cold cabbage, mixed with grated cheese, in a buttered baking or pie-dish, cover with a little melted butter and dredge with grated cheese and fine dry bread crumbs. Let it brown in the oven, and serve.

CHOUX DE BRUXELLES.
(Brussels Sprouts.)

Remove the outer leaves, parboil them, drain off, and put them into a saucepan with a large piece of butter, salt, and pepper, and chopped parsley. Serve hot.

Cold boiled Brussels sprouts make excellent salads when mixed with cold sliced potatoes.

CHOUX BROCOLIS.
(Broccoli Sprouts.)

Boil in salted water, drain them off, pour a sauce

à la crême over them (see p. 14), and serve hot. They may also be put warm into a salad-bowl and mixed with oil and vinegar.

CHOUCROUTE GARNIE.
(Garnished Sauerkraut.)

Wash and parboil some sauerkraut, strain it off, and cook it with a small bit of lean bacon, saveloys and Frankfurt sausages, and some stock, an onion stuck with cloves, and a bunch of herbs. When cooked, strain it off, and serve on a dish with the bacon cut into pieces, saveloys cut into slices, and the Frankfurt sausages left whole.

CAULIFLOWERS.

CHOUX-FLEURS EN SAUCE BLANCHE.
(Cauliflower with White Sauce.)

Cook the cauliflower in boiling water and a large quantity of salt, strain off, cover with thick white sauce, and serve.

CHOUX-FLEURS AU GRATIN.
(Cauliflower au gratin.)

Prepare and cook the cauliflower as in above recipe. Mix into some thick *sauce blanche* (see p. 12) two large spoonfuls of grated gruyère cheese. Butter a baking-dish, lay in the cauliflower broken in pieces and mixed with the *sauce blanche*, dredge with grated cheese, pour melted butter over the whole, dredge with fine bread crumbs, and brown in the oven.

CHOUX-FLEURS EN MARINADE.
(Cauliflower en Marinade.)

Parboil some cauliflower and break them into pieces. Dip each piece into a thick *sauce blanche* (see p. 12) so that it is entirely covered, and then into frying batter. Fry a light brown, and serve with fried parsley.

CHOUX-FLEURS EN SALADE.
(Cauliflower in Salad.)

Boil and strain off, break into pieces and serve in a salad-bowl while still warm with oil, vinegar, &c., and a little chopped parsley.

ENDIVE.

CHICORÉE AU JUS.
(Endives au Jus.)

Parboil some endives, strain them off, cut them in halves, season with pepper, tie in couples with fine string, and cook them in stock with a bunch of herbs; let the stock simmer slowly, then untie the endives, take them out, and serve them with a *roux* mixed with stock poured over them.

CHICORÉE À LA CRÊME.
(Endive with Crême.)

Parboil the endives, chop them up fine, put them into a saucepan with a large lump of fresh butter, some cream, a little powdered sugar, and some grated nutmeg. Stir during the whole process of cooking so as to bind the sauce, and serve.

CHICORÉE AU VELOUTÉ.
(Endive au Velouté.)

Same process as above recipe, but to the cream add the same quantity of rich gravy or stock.

CARROTS.

CAROTTES À LA MÉNAGÈRE.
(Carrots à la Ménagère.)

Cut some carrots into slices and cook them in stock mixed with white wine, peppercorns, a bunch of herbs, and parsley. When cooked, take out the peppercorns, herbs, and parsley, and bind the sauce with fresh butter and a little flour.

CAROTTES À LA MAÎTRE D'HÔTEL.
(Carrots à la Maître d'Hôtel.)

Parboil in water or stock with a little salt. Strain off and wipe, then fry in butter with chopped parsley, salt, and pepper.

Note.—For this recipe small round carrots or large carrots cut into slices.

CAROTTES À LA CRÊME.
(Carrots à la Crême.)

Parboil some round young carrots, strain them off, warm them up again in a sauce composed of fresh melted butter mixed with cream. Serve with grated nutmeg. A *sauce blanche* (see p. 12) may be substituted for the cream.

CAROTTES À LA FLAMANDE.
(Another Recipe for Carrots à la Crême.)

This dish is in season from the 1st May to the 1st October. Only small round carrots may be used.

Throw the carrots into boiling water and cook for five minutes; then throw them into cold water and remove the skins with a cloth. Put them into a saucepan with a very little water, a lump of butter, some salt, and sifted sugar. Cover the saucepan, and let the vegetables simmer for twenty minutes, turning the carrots from time to time so that they may be evenly cooked. When the carrots are quite soft, bind with two yolks of eggs, a large cupful of cream, a lump of butter, and half a teaspoonful of chopped parsley.

CAROTTES AU SUCRE.
(Carrots with Sugar.)

Boil some carrots, strain them off and mash them with a fork, add some milk and a little flour, sifted sugar, a spoonful of orange flower water, and the yolks of eggs; mix thoroughly, and add the whites of the eggs beaten into a froth and some fresh butter. Place the mixture into a deep pan or baking tin, and when cooked, serve on a hot dish. Sprinkle with sugar.

CELERY.

CÉLERI À LA MOUTARDE.
(Mustard Celery.)

Cut and split the celery into small pieces about two inches long, put it on to a *ravier* or side dish, or over it pour a *remoulade* sauce (see recipe, p. 18), in which a large spoonful of French mustard has been incorporated.

CELERI AU JUS À L'ESPAGNOLE.

Prepare the celery as *Cardons au maigre* (see recipe, p. 124), then cook it in some good *roux* mixed with strong stock or gravy. Serve hot.

CÉLERI FRIT.
(Fried Celery.)

Take two heads of celery, parboil them, cut them into pieces, let them soak a little in vinegar and salt, then dip them into batter and fry a deep yellow.

CÉLERI AU GRATIN.
(Celery au gratin.)

(See Cardons au Gratin, p. 124.)

CÉLERI RAVE.
(Celery Root or Bulb.)

This is sliced and prepared with mustard sauce. (See Céleri à la Moutarde.)

CÉLERI EN SALADE.
(Celery Salad.)

Cut two fine celery heads into thin strips about three inches long. Mix with chopped parsley and flavour with ordinary dressing.

MACÉDOINE DE LÉGUMES.
(Macedoine of Vegetables.)

Cut into pieces about an inch long and about half an inch thick equal quantities of carrots and turnips. To these add equal quantities of asparagus tops, green peas, French beans cut into pieces about an inch long, some pieces of cauliflower carefully broken up. Cook all together in a quart of water with a little salt, and strain through a coarse cloth. Put a large piece of butter into a saucepan; stir in a spoonful or two of flour and a tumblerful of stock, some salt, and a little powdered sugar. Cook for ten minutes; bind with the yolks of two eggs and a cupful of cream. Warm up the vegetables in this sauce, and mix carefully so as not to break them. Serve.

SALADS.

In French households salads are made not only from a variety of green vegetables, but also with many cooked vegetables, such as potatoes, beans, lentils, &c., either used separately or mixed together. The better known of these are—

Fresh Tomato Salad.
Cold Potato Salad.
Cold Haricots or Kidney Beans Salad.
Cold French Beans Salad.
Cold Boiled Lentil Salad.
Fresh Watercress Salad.
Fresh Cucumber Salad.
Cold Boiled Cauliflower Salad.
Cold Boiled Brussels Sprouts Salad.
Fresh Celery Salad.
Boiled Beetroot Salad.
Boiled Egg Plant Salad.

(See recipes of various vegetables.)

A mixture of fresh green salad, such as watercress, lettuce, or endive, and cooked vegetables often give an excellent result, such as cold sliced potatoes mixed with fresh endive or lettuce, with fresh sliced tomatoes or sliced cucumber. Shrimps and anchovies are also much used in fresh or vegetable salads.

(See Anchovy Salad, p. 34. See Beef Salad, p. 57. See Chicken Salad, p. 98.)

SALAD DE MACEDOINE.
(Macedoine Salad.)

The vegetables are prepared as for a *macedoine* (see Macedoine), and are served in a salad-bowl with *mayonnaise sauce* (see Sauces), or ordinary dressing.

SALADE DE CRESSON AND DE CERFEUIL.
(Salad of Watercress and Chervil.)

Equal quantities of cress and chervil are used with an ordinary dressing. This salad is most excellent with grouse.

SALADE DE MÂCHE.
(Corn Salad.)

This is seasonable in the autumn. Carefully wash and pick a pound of corn salad, slice a boiled beetroot, and cut a head of celery into small strips about an inch long. Mix these ingredients thoroughly together with the ordinary dressing.

SALADE JAPONAISE.
(Japanese Salad.)

Slice some cold boiled potatoes and put them into a salad-bowl with some mussels previously plainly cooked, shelled shrimps, stoned olives, boned anchovies, some slices of raw russet apples, some sliced *saucisson* carefully cut into strips, some chopped parsley, and chervil. Mix the ingredients thoroughly together with thick *mayonnaise* sauce. Garnish with thin slices of truffles.

SALADE JAPONAISE.
(A simpler recipe.)

A more simple Japanese salad may be made with sliced cold potatoes, mussels, sliced onions, and truffles. Mix with ordinary dressing.

SALADE RUSSE.
(Russian Salad.)

This is made like Japanese salad minus the sliced apples and mussels.

SALADE DE POISSON.
(Fish Salad.)

This is not made in a salad-bowl, but in a deep dish. The cold remains of any boiled fish may be used. The pieces of fish are boned and broken up into fragments about three inches square. Vegetables *en Macedoine* (see Macedoine of Vegetables) are placed in small heaps around the dish, alternating with the pieces of fish. Fresh sliced tomatoes are added, and chopped parsley. A mixture of vinegar and oil, salt, and pepper is then poured over the salad.

MACARONI.

MACARONI À LA FRANÇAISE.
(Macaroni—French style.)

Put a pound of macaroni into some boiling water, and cook it until soft with a small piece of butter, a little salt, and an onion stuck with cloves. Strain it off, and put it back into another saucepan with more butter, a quarter of a pound of grated gruyère cheese, the same quantity of grated parmesan, a little nutmeg, some peppercorns, and a few spoonfuls of fresh cream. Toss up the mixture several times during the process of cooking, and serve when the cheese become *stringy*.

MACARONI À L'ITALIENNE.
(Macaroni—Italian style.)

Cook the macaroni in salted water until quite soft; put a layer of the macaroni in a deep dish and cover with a layer of grated parmesan cheese; pour over some rich gravy or tomato sauce; add another layer of macaroni, cheese, and sauce, and before serving, pour over a little warm melted butter.

When the cheese becomes oily, the macaroni must be put back on to the fire and a little stock stirred in.

MACARONI AU GRATIN.

Boil some macaroni; strain it off; stir in a little grated gruyère and parmesan cheese. Heat the dish; dredge thoroughly with grated cheese and bread crumbs; add a few lumps of fresh butter, and brown in the oven.

TIMBALE DE MACARONI.
(Macaroni in Crust.)

Put the macaroni in salted water and strain it off; add pepper, butter, and equal quantities of grated gruyerè and parmesan cheese. Keep the macaroni on the fire until the cheese is melted, then butter a large mould, and line it with a thin coating of pastry such as is used for meat pies. Put in the macaroni prepared *à l'Italienne, i.e.*, mixed with tomato sauce or gravy and a few lumps of butter. Cover the mould over with paste; put a piece of buttered paper over the top. Cook in a hot oven for three-quarters of an hour or so, according to size. Slip the crust out of the mould and serve whole.

NOUILLES.

Nouilles are a species of macaroni cut into thin narrow strips.

NOUILLES AU GRATIN.

See recipe for Macaroni *au gratin* (page 169).

NOUILLES À L'ITALIENNE.

See recipe for Macaroni à l'Italienne (page 168).

Nouilles are also cooked *en Timbale* (see recipe), or with made dishes such as *Riz de veau à la Romaine* (see recipe).

RICE.

RIZ À LA MÉNAGÈRE.
(Rice à la Ménagère.)

Wash and boil some rice; strain it off, and cook it with some stock and some small dice of bacon previously browned in butter. Season with salt and pepper, and just before serving, pour over some tomato sauce (see recipe, p. 16).

SWEET DISHES.

Sweet dishes, or what are generally termed puddings, are not so common upon French tables as upon English. There are many excellent English recipes for puddings unknown in France. Stewed fruits or compôtes, boiled creams, &c., are the more usual *entremets sucrés*. Fine *patisserie* is rarely made at home in small households, and belongs to the confectioner's department. Here are a few recipes for ordinary French *entremets sucrés*.

COMPÔTE DE FRUIT.
(Stewed and Mashed Fruit.)

Various fruits, such as apples, pears, peaches, apricots, plums, greengages, rhubarb, &c., are excellent made *en compôte*, that is, thoroughly stewed down with sufficient sugar, and mashed with a fork or passed through a tammy. Sifted sugar is thickly dredged over the top, and mace, cloves, lemon peel, and vanilla are used for flavouring.

Apple *compôte* is specially good when served with a little currant jelly on the top.

MERINGUE APPLES.

Make a *compôte* of apples stewed in water and a little red wine. Beat up the whites of some eggs, mix in sufficient sifted sugar to make a thick paste. Spread this over the *compôte*, and brown in the oven. Serve.

POMMES AU BEURRE.
(Buttered Apples.)

Peel some fine russet apples and remove the cores; parboil them with some sugar, then strain off. Make a *compôte* of apples (see Compôtes), and line the bottom of a deep dish with it, covering the *compôte* with a thin layer of currant jelly. Then put in the parboiled russets, filling the hole of each apple with butter. Glaze with sifted sugar; brown in the oven, and serve with a preserved cherry or small quantity of jelly on each apple.

PRUNEAUX.
(Stewed Prunes.)

These are excellent when stewed in red wine, or, better still, a decoction of strong tea with sufficient sugar. Mace or vanilla must be used to flavour *pruneaux*.

PAIN AUX FRAMBOISES.
(Pair Raspberries.)

Take a small square tin loaf and slice off all the

crust. Boil up two pounds of fresh raspberries with sufficient sugar to form a thick syrup. Strain the mixture through a tammy, and pour it over the crumb-loaf in a deep glass dish. Let it cool and set for some hours, basting the loaf from time to time with the syrup, so that it may be thoroughly permeated, though not reduced to a shapeless "squash." Garnish with fresh cream, plain or whipped, and serve.

MONT-BLANC.
(Chestnuts and Cream.)

Take a pound of large chestnuts; remove the outer peel, and boil the chestnuts until quite tender. Remove the second peel, and press the chestnuts through a coarse tammy, reducing them to a dry *purée*. Serve them in a pyramid on a glass dish and garnish with whipped cream on the top of the pyramid and around it.

SOUFFLÉ-DE-RIZ.
(Rice Soufflé.)

Make a thick paste with some rice flour, powdered sugar, and some macaroons crushed into powder. Flavour with vanilla, coffee, chocolate, or lemon, &c. Add the yolks of four or five eggs, and the whites whisked into a stiff paste. Pour the mixture into a mould or deep pie-dish, dredge the top with sifted sugar, and cook under the salamander or in the oven.

PAIN-AU-RIZ.
(Rice Cake.)

Wash and boil half a pound of rice; strain it off, and cook it in a little boiled milk with pieces of lemon peel; let it cool, then stir in a pinch of fine salt, a quarter of a pound of sifted sugar, four whole eggs, and the yolks of four others, putting aside the whites. Butter a saucepan or mould, dredge in a few bread crumbs. Whisk up the whites of the eggs, and mix them gradually into the rice. Pour the mixture into the mould; cook for half an hour in the oven; take out of the mould, and serve.

ŒUFS À LA NEIGE.
(Snow Eggs.)

Boil some milk in a saucepan with some sifted sugar and a little orange flower water. Beat up the whites of six eggs to a very stiff consistency, and when the milk boils, put in the whisked whites one piece at a time, turning each piece with a skimmer, so that it may be cooked on both sides. Serve on a very hot dish; bind the milk with the yolks of four eggs; then pour it off into a deep dish; place in the pieces of white, and let the whole cool. Serve cold.

CRÊME À LA VANILLE.
(Vanilla Cream.)

Boil some milk or cream sweetened with powdered sugar, and flavour with small pieces of vanilla about half an inch long. Take the milk off the fire and let it cool; then mix in some yolks of eggs; strain the cream through a tammy, and let it set in a *bain-marie* over a moderate fire. Take out the pieces of vanilla. Let cool, and serve.

CRÊME À LA FLEUR-D'ORANGER.
(Orange Flower Water Cream.)

This is made like vanilla cream (see recipe), substituting orange flower water for vanilla.

Note.—Orange lemon or coffee cream may be made in the same manner as vanilla cream by substituting these flavourings for vanilla (see recipe).

CRÊME D'AMANDE.
(Almond Cream.)

Blanch two ounces of sweet almonds and three bitter almonds; pound in a mortar, and stir the almonds into some boiling cream. Pass through a tammy, and stir in the yolks of five eggs and two spoonfuls of orange flower water. Let the cream set in a *bain-marie*, and serve, garnished with a few burnt almonds.

CRÊME AU CHOCOLAT.
(Chocolate Cream.)

Take a pint of cream or milk, the yolks of three eggs, two ounces of chocolate, and five or six ounces of powdered sugar. Mix the cream and the sugar together, and let the mixture boil and simmer, then cool. Then stir in the eggs and the chocolate powdered very finely, and cook in the *bain-marie*.

CRÊME BRULÉE.

(Burnt Cream.)

Beat up the yolks of five eggs in a saucepan with a quarter of a teaspoonful of flour. Pour in a pint of milk drop by drop, stirring meanwhile; add a small piece of mace or some preserved lemon rind, half an ounce pounded pistachio nuts or almonds may also be added, with a few drops of orange flower water. Place the mixture on the fire, and stir continually so that the cream does not stick to the saucepan. When the cream is cooked, place a deep dish upon the stove containing a little powdered sugar and some water. Let the sugar brown slightly, then pour in the cream, and serve immediately.

CRÊME AU THÉ.

(Tea Cream.)

Boil up a pint of cream, and let it reduce; add a cupful of good tea made very strong, the yolks of three eggs, and sweeten to taste; mix them thoroughly; pass through a fine tammy; stir again, let cool, and serve.

BLANC-MANGER AU CAFÉ.
(Coffee Blancmange.)

Take two ounces of mocha coffee in beans, grind it, and put it into a glass of boiling water. Let it infuse, then pour off the clear coffee, leaving the dregs. To the coffee add seven or eight ounces of powdered sugar, and about one ounce of clear gelatine. Mix rather more than a pound of pounded almonds with three glassfuls of filtered water. Mix all together, pour into a mould; cook in the oven for half an hour, and serve cold.

MERINGUES À LA CRÊME.
(Cream Meringoes.)

Whisk up some whites of eggs with some powdered sugar, allowing one pound of sugar to twelve whites of eggs. When a thick paste is formed, spread some sheets of white paper upon a baking tray, and put a tablespoonful on the paper at intervals of about two inches; lightly dredge the meringues with finely crushed sugar, and cook in a slow oven. When the meringues are cooked, remove them carefully from the paper, and lightly crush in the centre with a teaspoon. Before serving fill the meringues two by two with whipped cream.

ENGLISH INDEX.

Almond cream, 176
Alose or shad au bleu, 42
Anchovy-butter with steak, 59
Anchovies à la Parisienne, 34
Artichokes à la bonne-femme, 119
,, ,, sauce poivrade, 119
,, ,, barigoule, 118
,, en fricassée de poulet, 119
,, with white sauce, 117
,, fritters à la Claire, 118
Asparagus tops au jus, 116
Aspic of fowl, 101

Bacon omelette, 54
Barbel à l'étuvée, 43
,, court-bouillon, 44
Beef-mode, 58
Beef-mode cold, 58
,, with sauce piquante, 57
Beetroot à la Chartreuse, 122
,, ,, crême, 122
,, ,, Poitevine, 122
,, -salad, 122
Blanquette of lamb, 88
,, veal, 70
Blown potatoes, 147
Boiled beef, 57
Braised leg of mutton, 78
,, ox tongue, 64
,, plovers, 114
,, rump of beef with tomato sauce, 63
Braised sturgeon, 39
Breast of veal au blanc, 70

Breast of veal with green peas, 69
Brill in pickle, 22
,, à la Provençale, 23
Broad beans, 146
,, ,, en purée, 146
Broccoli sprouts, 156
Broiled larks, 111
,, whiting, 31
Brown sauce, 12
Brussels sprouts, 156
Burnt cream, 177
Buttered apples, 173

Cabbage-soup, 4
Cabbage au gratin, 156
,, with bacon, 155
Calf's head sauce pauvre-homme, 68
,, ,, en tortue, 69
,, foot à la Poulette, 73
,, liver braised à l'Italienne, 71
,, ,, à la Bourgeoise, 72
,, tongue à l'étuvée, 72
Capilotade of turkey, 89
Capsicum or sweet Chilian hors d'œuvre, 125
Carbonade of mutton, 79
Cardoons au maigre, 123
,, ,, gras, 123
,, ,, gratin, 123
,, à l'Italienne, 125
,, à la Poulette, 125
Carp au bleu, 43
Carrot-soup, 9
Carrots à la Ménagère, 161

Carrots à la crême, 161
,, ,, Maître d'hôtel, 161
,, with sugar, 162
Cauliflowers in marinade, 158
,, ,, salad, 159
,, au gratin, 158
,, with white sauce, 158
Celery au gratin, 163
,, root or bulb, 164
,, salad, 164
Chaud-froid of chicken, 101
Cheese-fondu, 55
,, eggs, 50
,, omelette, 54
Chestnuts and cream, 174
,, in purée, 147
Chicken-chasseur, 96
,, -Villeroy, 96
,, -salad, 98
,, à la Marengo, 97
,, ,, Macédoine, 97
,, in marinade, 98
,, stewed with green peas, 97
Chocolate cream, 176
Civet of hare, 107
Cod fish, 29
,, Béchamel, 29
,, croquettes, 30
,, in brandade, 30
,, with black butter, 30
Coffee blancmange, 178
Cold venison, 107
,, roast turkey sauce Robert, 89
Conger eel, 35
Corn salad, 166
Crab soup, 11
Crayfish soup, 10
,, court-bouillon, 46
,, à la Bordelaise, 46
Cream méringues, 178
Cream and sorrel soup, 5
Cress, 144
Croûte-au-pôt soup, 2
Cucumber au blanc, 151
,, à l'Italienne, 151
,, -salad, 152
Cutlets of veal à la Milanaise, 76

DRIED herrings as hors d'œuvre, 34
,, peas, 134
Duck with turnips, 103
,, ,, green peas, 103
,, ,, olives, 104
,, en salmis, 104

EGG-plant à la Provençale, 120 and 121
Eggs on the stit, 48
,, with mustard sauce, 49
,, à l'Aurore, 50
,, with French sausages and tomato sauce, 50
,, à la tripe, 51
,, Béchamel, 52
Eels à la Tartare, 21
Endives au jus, 160
,, à la crême, 160
,, au velouté, 160

FILLET with mushrooms, 59
,, ,, olives, 60
,, Financière, 60
,, à l'Allemande, 60
,, Jardinière, 60
,, Bordelaise, 60
,, à l'Italienne, 61
,, à la Portugaise, 61
,, ,, Provençale, 61
,, ,, Créole, 61
,, ,, Printanière, 61
,, sauce Madère, 62
,, purée de légumes, 62
Filleted pike Béchamel, 42
,, soles à l'Orly, 25
Fish soup, 9
,, salad, 167
Fore-quarter of lamb, 87
Fowl with tarragon, 95
,, in the pot, 91
,, with onions, 91
,, ,, rice, 92
,, godard, 92
,, Montmorency, 93

Fowl-Bourguignonne, 99
,, à la bonne-femme, 99
,, ,, sauce tomate, 100
,, au blanc, 100
French beans and scarlet-runners, 139-140
French beans à la Poulette, 140
,, ,, ,, Lyonnaise, 140
Fresh herrings and mustard sauce, 33
Fresh-water fish, 39
Fricassée of chicken or fowl, 94
Fried celery, 163
,, pigeons, 106
,, sheep's brains, 82
,, calf's liver, 71
,, eggs with tomatoes and onions, 49
,, tench, 45
,, pilchards, 35
,, salmon, 41
,, tunny, 28
,, skate, 27
,, artichokes, 118
,, egg-plant, 120
,, carp, 21
,, salsifies, 135
,, beef kidney, 65
Fritots of chicken, 100
Frogs à la Poulette, 46

Garnished sauerkraut, 157
Gibelotte of young rabbit, 109
Giblets chipolata, 90
Glazed knuckle of beef, 63
,, onions, 128
,, turnips, 149
Green beans fried in butter, 141
,, haricot beans Maître d'hôtel, 141
Green peas with cream, 133
,, ,, à la parisienne, 133
,, ,, with bacon or ham, 133
Grey mullet Maître d'hôtel, 23
,, ,, with Dutch sauce, 23
Grilled tunny, 28

Grilled alose or shad with sorrel, 42
,, barbel, 44
,, artichokes à la Provençale, 117

Haricot of mutton, 84
Hard boiled eggs and sorrel, 52
Hare en daube, 108
Herb soup, 7

Italian paste soup, 3

John Dory court-bouillon, 42
Julienne soup, 3

Kidney omelette, 54
,, beans with bacon, 142
Knuckle of veal in gelée, 76

Lamb cutlets à l'Italienne, 87
,, ,, with fresh vegetables, 88
Leek and potato soup, 7
Leg of mutton with stewed lettuce, 82
Leg of mutton with hearts of artichokes, 82
Leg of mutton as venison, 78
,, ,, de sept heures, 80
,, ,, with white beans, 80
,, ,, ,, mushroom, 80
,, ,, ,, lentils, 81
,, ,, à la Financière, 81
,, ,, with carrots, 81
,, ,, à la Jardinière, 81
,, ,, with tomatoes, 81
Lentils, 144
Lettuces stewed in gravy, 126
Liver of beef with carrots and onions, 67
Lobster à l'Américaine, 37
,, à la Provençale, 37
Lyonnaise omelette, 55

English Index.

MACARONI, 168
,, soup,
Mackerel Maître d'hôtel, 32
,, with gooseberries, 32
Macédoine of vegetables, 164
,, salad, 166
Maître d'hôtel sauce, 13
Mashed potatoes, 131
,, onions à la Soubise, 127
Matelote of barbel, carp, eels, 22
Mayonnaise, 36
Melted butter, 13
Meringue apples, 173
Milk soup, 6
Miroton beef, 56
Mixed beans, 142
Moril mushrooms, 154
Mornay shells, 28
Mushrooms à la Provençale, 153
,, ,, Poulette, 154
,, on toast, 154
Mushroom omelette, 54
Mussels à la Poulette, 38
,, ,, Provençale, 38
,, ,, Marinière, 39
Mustard celery, 163
Mutton cutlets, 82
,, goulache, 85

NEW white beans Maître d'hôtel, 141

OMELETTE with herbs, 53
Onion soup, 6
Onions en ragoût, 127
Orange flower water cream, 175
Ortolans, 115
Ox tongue au gratin, 64
,, papillotes, 64
,, sauce piquante, 65
,, with sauerkraut, 65
,, and mashed potatoes, 65
Ox brains with black butter, 66
,, Maître d'hôtel, 66
,, Mayonnaise, 66
,, Printanière, 66

PAIR raspberries, 173
Partridge à l'estoufade, 110
,, with cabbage, 110
Pickled oysters, 38
Pigeons à la Crapaudine, 105
,, stewed with green peas, 105
,, ,, ,, asparagus, 106
Pike au bleu, 42
Plovers au gratin, 114
Potato straws, 147
,, soup, 8
,, salad, 132
Potatoes in jackets, 129
,, Maître d'hôtel, 130
,, à la Parisenne, 130
,, ,, sauce blanche, 130
,, au lard, 130
,, with cream, 131
Poultry, 89
Pumpkin soup, 8
Purée of potatoes with cheese, 131
,, ,, white beans, 142
,, ,, green peas, 134
,, ,, lentils, 144

QUAILS with green peas, 113
,, ,, stewed lettuce, 113

RABBIT sauté, 109
Red bean soup, 5
Rice soup, 2
,, à la Ménagère, 171
,, soufflé, 174
,, cake, 175
Rissoles of spinach, 145
,, ,, beef, 57
Roast sturgeon, 39
,, salmon, 41
Roasted lobster, 36
Roast quails, 113
Roasted snipe, 112
Roast plovers, 114
,, thrush, 115
Russian salad, 167

English Index.

SALAD of boiled beef, 57
,, ,, white beans, 143
,, ,, French ,, 143
,, ,, watercress and chervil, 166
Salmis of pheasant, 110
,, ,, larks, 111
,, ,, snipe chasseur, 112
,, ,, ,, in chaffing dish, 112
,, ,, thrushes, 115
Salsifies with white sauce, 135
,, ,, cream, 135
,, ,, anchovy butter, 136
Salt cod fish, 30
Sauté fowl, 92
Scallop of veal Milanaise, 76
Scrambled eggs, 51
Semolina and sorrel soup, 3
Sheep's brains au gratin, 83
,, ,, Mayonnaise, 83
,, ,, in blanquette, 83
,, trotters Lyonnaise, 85
,, ,, Poulette, 84
,, ,, sauce Robert, 85
Sirloin of fillet of beef stewed, 62
,, ,, ,, with celery, 62
Skate Ste. Ménéhould, 26
,, sauce blanche, 26
,, with black butter, 27
Sliced haunch of venison, St. Hubert, 107
Slices of roast fillet with celery, 62
Smoked salmon, 41
Snow eggs, 175
Sorrel omelette, 54
,, in purée au gras, 137
,, ,, ,, maigre, 137
Soufflé of chicken, 102
Spinach Maître d'hôtel, 145
,, à l'Ancienne, 145
St. Germain soup, 5
St. Jacques shells, 27
Stewed prunes, 173
,, and mashed fruit, 172
Stuffed fowl in jelly, 94
,, tomatoes, 138
,, cucumbers, 151
,, cabbage, 155

Sturgeon court-bouillon, 40
,, in fricandeau, 40
,, ,, matelote, 40
Sweet dishes, 172
,, potato fritters, 132
,, potatoes with butter, 132
Sweetbreads à la Poulette, 73
,, with sorrel, 74
,, à la Financière, 74
,, in fricandeau, 74
,, ,, papillotes, 75

TEA cream, 177
Teal, 113
,, with olives, 114
Tench à la Poulette, 44
,, court-boullion, 45
Thrush, 115
Tomato salad, 138
,, omelette, 54
,, soup, 8
Tripe mode de Caen, 75
Trout grillée, 43
Tunny fish, 28
,, in fricandeau, 29
Turkey in daube, 89
Turnip soup, 6
Turnips Béchamel, 148
,, au jus, 148
,, in purée, 148
,, la Poulette, 149
,, with sugar, 150

VANILLA cream, 175
Veal soup, 11
Veal, 68
Vermicelli soup, 4

WEAVER or perch, 33
Whitings au gratin, 31
,, and sweet herbs, 31
White sauce, 12

YOUNG rabbit with tomato sauce, 110

FRENCH INDEX

ABATIS de dinde, 90
  ,, ,, chipolata, 90
Alose au bleu, 42
  ,, grillée à l'oseille, 42
Anchois à la Parisienne, 34
Anguilles à la tartare, 21
Artichauts à la Barigoule, 118
  ,, ,, bonne-femme, 119
  ,, en fricassée de poulet, 119
Artichauts frits, 118
  ,, grillés à la Provençale, 117
Artichauts sauce blanche, 117
  ,, ,, poivrade à l'huile, 119
Aspic de volaille, 101
Aubergines à la Provençale, 120
  ,, farcies, 120
  ,, frites, 120

BARBILLON à l'étuvée, 43
  ,, court-bouillon, 44
  ,, grillée, 44
Barbue marinée, 22
  ,, Provençale, 23
Bécasses rôties, 112
Beignets de patates, 132
  ,, d'artichauts à la Claire, 118
Betteraves à la crême, 122
  ,, ,, Poitevine, 122
  ,, en salade, 122
  ,, à la Chartreuse, 122
Beurre-fondu ; beurre noir, 13

Bifteck beurre d'anchois, 59
Blanc-mange au café, 178
Blanquette d'agneau, 88
  ,, de veau, 70
Bœuf au gratin, 57
  ,, en salade, 57
  ,, miroton, 56
  ,, -mode, 58
  ,, ,, froid, 58
  ,, sauce piquante, 57
Bouillabaisse, 9
Bouillon de veau, 11
Boulettes de bœuf, 57
Brochet au bleu, 42

CABILLAUD Béchamel, 29
Cailles aux laitues, 113
  ,, ,, petits-pois, 103
  ,, rôties, 113
Canard aux olives, 104
  ,, ,, navets, 103
  ,, ,, petits-pois, 103
Capilotade de dinde, 89
Carbonade de mouton, 79
Cardons à l'Italienne, 125
  ,, à la Poulette, 125
  ,, au gras, 124
  ,, ,, gratin, 124
  ,, ,, maigre, 124
Carottes à la crême, 161
  ,, ,, Flamande, 162
  ,, ,, Ménagère, 161
  ,, au sucre, 162
  ,, Maître-d'hôtel, 161

French Index. 185

Carpe au bleu, 43
,, frite, 21
Céleri au gratin, 163
,, ,, jus, 163
,, en salade, 164
,, frit, 163
,, à la moutarde, 163
,, -rave, 164
Cervelle de bœuf, beurre noir, 66
,, ,, Maître d'hôtel, 66
,, ,, Mayonnaise, 66
,, ,, Printanière, 66
Cervelles de mouton frites, 82
,, ,, au gratin, 82
,, ,, en blanquette, 83
Cervelles de mouton Mayonnaise, 66
Champignons à la Provençale, 153
,, ,, Poulette, 154
Chaud-froid de volaille, 101
Chicorée à la crème, 160
,, au jus, 160
,, ,, velonté, 160
Chou au lard, 155
,, ,, gratin, 156
,, ,, brocolis, 156
,, de Buxelles, 156
,, farci, 155
Choux-fleurs au gratin, 158
,, on marinade, 158
,, ,, salade, 159
,, ,, sauce blanche, 158
Choucroute garnie, 157
Civet de lièvre, 107
Compôte de fruit, 172
Concombres à l'Italienne, 151
,, en salade, 151
,, farcis, 151
Congre, 35
Coquilles St. Jacques, 27
,, à la Mornay, 28
Cotelettes d'agneau à l'Italienne, 87
,, ,, aux légumes frais, 88
Côtelettes de mouton jardinière, 82
,, en demi-deuil, 88
,, de veau Milanaise, 76

Court-bouillon, 20
Crême au chocolat, 176
,, ,, thé, 177
,, brûlée, 177
,, d'amande, 176
,, fleur d'oranger, 176
,, vanille, 175
Croquettes de cabillaud, 29
Croûtes aux champignons, 154
Culotte de bœuf braisé purée de tomates, 63

DINDE en daube, 89
Dorade court-bouillon, 42

ECREVISSES court-bouillon, 46
,, Bordelaise, 46
Epaule de mouton en ballon, 79
Epinards à l'ancienne, 145
,, au jus, 146
,, Maître d'hôtel, 145
Escalope de veau Milanaise, 76
Esturgeon braisé, 39
,, court-bouillon, 40
,, en matelote, 40
,, ,, fricandeau, 40
,, rôti, 39

FÈVES à la crême, 146
Filet à l'Allemande, 60
,, ,, Italienne, 61
,, à la Provençale, 61
,, aux olives, 60
,, ,, champignons, 59
,, Bordelaise, 60
,, Créole, 61
,, Financière, 60
,, Jardinière, 60
,, de bœuf, 59
,, Portugaise, 61
,, Printanière, 61
,, purée de légumes, 62
,, sauce Madère, 62
,, de soles à l'Orly, 25
,, de brochet Béchamel, 42

Fondu au fromage, 55
Foie de bœuf aux carottes and aux oignons, 67
Foie de veau à la Bourgeoise, 72
,, ,, ,, sauté à l'Italienne, 71
Fricassée de poulet, 94
Fritots, 100

GIBELOTTE de lapereaux, 80
Gigot aux carottes, 81
,, ,, champignons, 80
,, ,, haricots, 80
,, ,, lentilles, 81
,, ,, tomates, 81
,, -chevreuil, 78
,, aux cœurs de laitues, 82
,, ,, ,, d'artichauts, 82
,, de mouton braisé, 78
,, ,, sept-heures, 80
,, Jardinière, 81
,, Financière, 81
Goulache, 85
Grenouilles à la Poulette, 46
Grive rôtie, 115

HARENGS frais sauce moutarde, 33
,, secs en hors d'œuvre, 34
Haricots blancs frais Maître d'hôtel, 141
Haricots de mouton, 84
,, flageolets Maître d'hôtel, 141
Haricots panachés, 142
,, -Soissons au lard, 142
,, verts à la Lyonnaise, 140
,, ,, ,, Poulette, 140
,, sautés au beurre, 141
Homard à l'Amèricaine, 37
,, à la broche, 36
,, ,, Provençale, 37
,, court-bouillon, 35
,, sauce mayonnaise, 36
Huîtres marinées, 38

LAITUES au jus, 126
Langue de bœuf au gratin, 64
,, ,, ,, braisé, 64
,, ,, ,, choucroute, 65
,, ,, ,, papillotes, 64
,, ,, purée de pommes de terre, 65
Langue de bœuf sauce piquante, 65
,, ,, ,, veau à l'étuvée, 72
Lapereaux sauce tomate, 110
Lapin sauté, 109
Lièvre en daube, 108

MACARONI à la Française, 168
,, à l'Italienne, 168
,, au gratin, 169
Macédoine de légumes, 164
Maquereaux aux groseilles, 32
,, Maître d'hôtel, 32
Matelote de carpe and d'anguille, 22
,, ,, barbillon, 22
Mauviettes rôties, 111
Méringues à la crême, 178
Merlans au gratin, 31
,, aux fines herbes, 31
,, grillés, 31
Mont-blanc, 174
Morilles sautées, 154
Morue au beurre noir, 30
,, en brandade, 30
Moules à la Marinière, 39
,, ,, Poulette, 38
,, ,, Provençale, 38
Mulets Maître d'hôtel, 23
,, sauce hollandaise, 23

NAVETS à la Poulette, 149
,, au jus, 148
,, ,, sucre, 150
,, Béchamel, 148
,, glacés, 149
Noix-de-bœuf à la gelée, 63
,, ,, -veau ,, ,, 76
Nouilles à l'Italienne, 170
,, au gratin, 170

French Index.

Œufs à l'aurore, 50
,, à l'oseille, 52
,, à la tripe, 51
,, au fromage, 50
,, aux saucisses and sauce tomate, 50
Œufs Béchamel, 52
,, brouillés, 51
,, dūrs à l'oseille, 52
,, frits aux tomates and aux oignons, 49
Œufs-miroir, 48
,, -neige, 175
,, pochés au consommé, 49
,, sauce moutarde, 49
Oignons farcis, 127
,, glacés, 128
Omelette à l'oseille, 54
,, au fromage, 54
,, ,, lard, 53
,, aux champignons, 54
,, ,, fines-herbes, 53
,, ,, tomates, 54
,, ,, rognons de mouton, 54
,, Lyonnaise, 55
Ortolans, 115

Pain aux framboises, 173
,, au riz, 173
Patates au beurre, 132
Perdrix à l'Estoufade, 110
,, aux choux, 110
Petits-pois, à la crême, 133
,, ,, Parisienne, 133
,, au lard and au jambon, 133
Pieds de mouton à la Lyonnaise, 85
,, ,, ,, Poulette, 84
,, ,, ,, sauce Robert, 85
,, veau à la Poulette, 73
Pigeons à la Crapaudine, 105
,, aux petits-pois, 105
,, ,, pointes d'asperges, 106
,, frits, 106
Piments en hors d'œuvre, 125
Pluviers au gratin, 114

Pluviers braisés, 114
,, rôtis, 114
Pointes d'asperges au jus, 116
Pois-chiches, 134
Poitrine de veau au blanc, 70
,, ,, aux petits-pois, 69
Pommes au beurre, 173
,, de terre à la crême, 130
,, ,, ,, Parisienne, 130
,, ,, au lard, 130
,, ,, en salade, 132
,, ,, en robe de chambre, 129
Pommes de terre en sauce blanche, 130
Pommes de terre Maître d'hôtel, 130
Pommes-pailles, 147
Pommes soufflées, 147
Pot-au-feu, 1
Potage au riz, 2
,, crôute au pot, 2
,, à l'oignon, 6
,, au potiron, 8
,, aux crabes, 11
,, ,, pommes de terre et poireaux, 7
Potage aux herbes, 7
,, bisque, 10
,, crême d'oseille, 5
,, Julienne, 3
,, macaroni, 4
,, pâtes d'Italie, 3
,, purée de carottes, 9
,, ,, navets, 6
,, ,, haricots rouges au riz, 5
Potage Parmentier, 8
,, semoule et oseille, 3
,, St. Germain, 5
Poularde farcie à la gelée, 94
,, Godard, 92
,, Montmorency, 93
Poule-au-pot, 91
,, -riz, 92
,, aux oignons, 91
Poulet à l'estragon, 96
,, la Bourguignonne, 99

Poulet à la bonne-femme, 99
,, au blanc, 100
,, aux petits-pois, 97
,, -chasseur, 99
,, en marinade, 98
,, ,, salade, 98
,, Macédoine, 97
,, Marengo, 97
,, saute, 92
,, sauce tomate, 100
,, -Villeroy, 96
Pruneaux, 173
Purée de fèves, 146
,, ,, marrons, 147
,, ,, navets, 148
,, ,, haricots blancs, 142
,, ,, lentilles, 144
,, d'oignons à la Soubise, 127
,, d'oseille au gras, 137
,, ,, ,, maigre, 137
,, de petits-pois, 134
,, ,, pommes de terre, 131

QUARTIER d'agneau à la Bernoise, 87
,, ,, farci, 87

RAGOÛT d'oignons, 127
Raie Ste. Ménéhould, 26
,, au beurre noir, 27
,, frite, 27
,, sauce blanche, 26
Rémoulade chaude, 18
Ris-de-veau à l'oseille, 74
,, ,, en fricandeau, 74
,, ,, ,, papillotes, 75
,, ,, à la Poulette, 73
,, ,, financière, 74
Rissoles de bœuf, 57
,, d'épinards, 145
Riz à la Ménagère, 171
Rognon de bœuf sauté, 65
Rouelles de cerf à la St. Hubert, 107
Roux, 12

SALADE de poisson, 167
,, russe, 167
,, de haricots blancs, 145
,, ,, ,, verts, 143
,, ,, Macédoine, 166
,, ,, cresson et de cerfeuil, 166
Salade de mâche, 166
,, d'aubergines à la Provençale, 121
Salade japonaise, 166
,, d'anchois, 34
Salmis de faisan, 110
,, ,, mauviettes, 111
,, ,, bécasses au chasseur, 112
,, ,, ,, à l'esprit-de-vin, 112
Salmis de grives, 115
,, ,, canard, 104
Salsifis à la crème, 135
,, au beurre d'anchois, 136
,, ,, jus, 136
,, en sauce blanche, 135
,, frits, 135
Sarcelles, 113
,, aux olives, 114
Sardines fraîches, 35
Sauce blanche, 12
,, Maître d'hôtel, 13
,, liée Maître d'hôtel, 13
,, hollandaise, 13
,, crême, 14
,, Béchamel maigre, 14
,, ,, grasse, 14
,, à la Duxelle, 14
,, piquante, 15
,, ravigotte, 15
,, Italienne, 15
,, poivrade, 15
,, au beurre d'anchois, 16
,, Robert, 16
,, Poulette, 17
,, verte, 17
,, tartare ou remoulade, 17
,, mayonnaise, 13
,, à l'huile, 18
,, indienne, 19
,, béarnaise, 19

Saumon fumé, 41
,, rôti, 41
,, sauté, 41
Soles Marguery, 24
,, à la Parisienne, 25
,, au gratin, 25
,, en matelote normande, 24
Soufflés de volaille, 102
Soufflé de riz, 174
Soupe au lait, 6
,, aux choux, 4

TANCHE à la Poulette, 44
,, grillée, 45
,, court-bouillon, 45
Tanches frites, 45
Tête de veau sauce pauvre-homme, 68

Tête de veau en tortue, 69
Thon, 28
,, frit, 28
,, grillé, 28
,, en fricandeau, 29
Timbale de macaroni, 169
Tomates farcies, 138
,, en salade, 138
Tranche de filet rôti au céleri, 62
,, ,, bœuf, sauté, 62
Tripes mode de Caen, 75
Truite court-bouillon, 43

VIVE ou perche Maître d'hôtel, 33
,, ,, ,, à la Normande, 33
,, ,, ,, ,, Bordelaise, 33